THE GREAT HOPE

E. G. White

Adapted from *The Great Controversy*

Pacific Press® Publishing Association
Nampa, Idaho

Review and Herald® Publishing Association
Hagerstown, Maryland

A NOTE FOR YOU . . .

What does it take to live with hope amid epic-sized natural disasters, wars, terrorism, nuclear proliferation, political revolutions, constant awareness of global pain, and dizzying in formation overload?

While facing a future with so many unknowns, we need reminding of the old maxim "Those who cannot remember the past are condemned to repeat it." But what will help us remember the past? Some wisdom from Albert Einstein comes to our aid: our great need for "holy curiosity." Such a curiosity will drive us to understand our present and future in the light of our past.

The book you have is a sampling from *The Great Controversy,* a time-tested classic of both history and prophecy—exploring what God will do in the future in light of His past interaction with humanity. Although written more than a century ago, the insights found in *The Great Hope* offer cutting-edge direction for the twenty-first century. Its author, Ellen G. White, is considered the most widely translated American author, with one of her many books having been translated into more than 160 languages.

Generous donors made it possible for you to have a personal copy of *The Great Hope.*

Why?

Because it changed their lives for the better, and they believe it could change your life, too.

Why?

Because in these chapters you will travel in time through human history, from humanity's beginning until Jesus Christ's promised return. On this adventure you will:

- find out what Christ offered to save us
- discover truths that will protect you from Satan's lies
- come to understand life-changing spiritual realities
- sense God's interplay in the cosmic history and where you fit in
- catch a glimpse of the most glorious picture ever portrayed to the human mind—the end of the human experience as we know it and the beginning of . . .

Well, we shouldn't tell you how the book ends, because with "holy curiosity" you can discover it for yourself!

Chapter 1

WHY IS THERE SUFFERING?

Many see the work of evil, with its pain and loss, and question how this can exist under the rulership of One who is infinite in wisdom, power, and love. Those who are inclined to doubt take this as an excuse for rejecting the words of the Bible. Tradition and wrong interpretations have clouded the Bible's teaching about God's character, the nature of His government, and the principles of how He deals with sin.

It is impossible to explain the origin of sin in a way that gives a reason for its existence. Yet we can understand enough about sin's beginning and final end to show clearly God's justice and goodness. In no way was God responsible for sin. He did not remove His divine grace; nor was there anything lacking in the divine government that provided a cause for the rebellion. Sin is an intruder for whose presence no one can give a reason. To excuse it is to defend it. If we could find an excuse for it, it would no longer be sin. Sin is the expression of a principle that is at war with the law of love, which is the foundation of God's government.

Before sin began, there was peace and joy everywhere in the universe. Love for God was supreme, love for one another unselfish. Christ the Only Begotten of God was one with the eternal Father in nature, in character, and in purpose—the only being who could enter into all the counsels and plans of God. "By Him all things were created that are in heaven . . . , whether thrones or dominions or principalities or powers" (Colossians 1:16).

Since the law of love is the foundation of God's government, the happiness of all created beings depended on their willing harmony with its principles of righteousness. God takes no pleasure in forced allegiance, and He grants everyone freedom of will, so that they can choose to serve Him voluntarily.

But one of God's created beings chose to misuse this freedom. Sin originated with an angel who, next to Christ, had been the being God honored the most. Before his fall, Lucifer was chief of the covering cherubs, holy and pure. "Thus says the Lord God: 'You were the seal of perfection, full of wisdom and perfect in beauty. You were in Eden, the garden of God; every precious stone was your covering. . . . You were the anointed cherub who covers; I established you; you were on the holy mountain of God; you walked back and forth in the midst of fiery stones. You were perfect in your ways from the day you were created, till iniquity was found in you. . . . Your heart was lifted up because of your beauty; you corrupted your wisdom for the sake of your splendor'" (Ezekiel 28:12-17). "You have set your heart as the heart of a god" (verse 6). "You have said . . . , 'I will exalt my throne above the stars of God; I will also sit on the mount of the congregation . . . ; I will ascend above the heights of the clouds, I will be like the Most High'" (Isaiah 14:13, 14).

Coveting the honor that the Father had given His Son, this prince of angels wanted the power that was Christ's alone to use. A note of discord now marred heaven's harmonies. Seeing someone exalt himself gave the other angels, who held God's glory as supreme, a strange dread of something evil. The heavenly councils pleaded with Lucifer. The Son of God showed him the goodness and justice of the Creator and the sacred nature of His law. In rejecting it, Lucifer would dishonor his Maker and bring ruin on himself. But the warning only stirred his resistance. Lucifer allowed his jealousy of Christ to control him.

Pride fed his desire for supremacy. The high honors God had given Lucifer did not make him grateful to the Creator. He wanted to be equal with God. Yet everyone recognized that the Son of God was the Ruler of heaven, one with the Father in power and authority. Christ participated in all the counsels of God, but Lucifer was not allowed to enter into the divine plans. This mighty angel questioned, "Why should Christ have the supremacy? Why is He honored like this above Lucifer?"

Discontent Among the Angels

Leaving his place in God's presence, Lucifer went out to spread discontent among the angels. With mysterious secrecy, hiding his real purpose under an appearance of reverence for God, he tried to make the angels dissatisfied with the laws that governed heavenly beings. He suggested that these laws were unnecessary and held them back. Since their natures were holy, he urged that angels should follow their own wills. God had dealt unfairly with him by giving supreme honor to Christ. He claimed he was not trying to exalt himself but was seeking to win liberty for every being in heaven, so that each one could reach a higher level of existence.

God was patient with Lucifer. He did not remove him from his honored position even when he began to make false claims to the angels. Again and again God offered him pardon if he would repent and submit. To convince him of his error, God made efforts that only infinite love could devise. Discontent had never before been known in heaven. At first, Lucifer himself did not understand the real nature of his feelings. As God showed that there was no reason for his dissatisfaction, Lucifer was convinced that the divine claims were right and that he ought to acknowledge them to all heaven. If he had done this, he would have saved himself and many angels. If he had been willing to return to God, satisfied to fill the place God had given him, God would have reinstated him to his position. But pride would not let him submit. He claimed that he did not need to repent, and he fully committed himself to the great controversy against his Maker.

He now applied all the powers of his master mind to deception, to gain the sympathy of the angels. Satan claimed that God had judged him wrongly and had restricted his liberty. After misrepresenting Christ's words, he moved on to telling actual lies, accusing the Son of God of plotting to humiliate him before the inhabitants of heaven.

All whom he could not win to his side he accused of being indifferent to the concerns of heavenly beings. He resorted to misrepresenting the Creator. He tried to perplex the angels with subtle arguments about God's plans. Everything simple he shrouded in mystery, and by clever perversion he made the plainest statements of God appear doubtful. His high position gave greater credibility to his claims. He persuaded many to join him in rebellion.

Disaffection Ripens Into Active Revolt

God in His wisdom allowed Satan to carry on his work, until the spirit of dissent ripened into revolt. It was necessary for God to allow him to develop his plans fully, so that anyone could see their true nature. Lucifer was greatly loved by the heavenly beings, and his influence over them was strong. God's government included the inhabitants not only of heaven, but of all the worlds He had created. Satan thought that if he could bring the angels with him in rebellion, he could also bring the other worlds. Using false reasoning and fraud, he had great power to deceive. Even the loyal angels could not fully discern his character or see where his work was leading.

Satan had been so highly honored, and he had cloaked all his actions with so much mystery, that it was difficult to show the angels the true nature of his work. Sin would not appear to be the evil thing it was until it was fully developed. Holy beings could not recognize what would be the results of setting aside God's law. At first Satan claimed to be trying to promote God's honor and the good of all of heaven's inhabitants.

In His response to sin, God could use only righteousness and truth. Satan could use what God could not—flattery and deceit. Everyone needed to understand the true character of this angel who wanted God's position. He must have time to reveal himself by his evil works.

Satan blamed God for the discord that his own actions had caused in heaven. He declared that all evil was the result of God's government. So it was necessary that he demonstrate how his proposed changes in God's law would work out. His own acts must condemn him. The whole universe must see the deceiver unmasked.

Even after deciding that Satan could no longer remain in heaven, Infinite Wisdom did not destroy him. The loyalty of God's creatures must rest on the conviction that He is just and fair. The inhabitants of heaven and of other worlds were not prepared to understand the consequences of sin, so they could not then have seen the justice and mercy of God if He had destroyed Satan at that time. If God had blotted him out of existence immediately, they would have served God from fear rather than from love. God would not have fully destroyed the deceiver's influence nor wiped out the spirit of rebellion. For the good of the universe through eternal ages, Satan must develop his principles more fully. Then all created beings would be able to see his charges against the divine government in their true light.

Satan's rebellion was to be a testimony to the universe about the terrible results of sin. His rule would show the fruit of setting aside God's authority. The history of this terrible experiment of rebellion would be a safeguard forever to all holy beings to save them from sin and its punishment.

When the announcement came that the great usurper must be expelled from heaven with all his sympathizers, the rebel leader boldly swore his contempt for the Creator's law. He denounced the divine statutes as a restriction of liberty and declared his intention to abolish all law. Freed from this restraint, he claimed, the inhabitants of heaven could achieve a higher state of existence.

Banished From Heaven

Satan and his followers threw the blame for their rebellion on Christ. They declared that if they had not been rebuked, they would never have rebelled. Stubborn and defiant, yet blasphemously claiming to be innocent victims of oppressive power, the chief rebel and his sympathizers were banished from heaven (see Revelation 12:7-9).

Satan's spirit still inspires rebellion on earth in unrepentant people. Like him they promise liberty through violating God's law. Condemning sin still stirs up hatred. Satan leads people to justify themselves and to try to get the sympathy of others in their sin. Instead of correcting their errors, they spread resentment of the one who points out their sin, as if that individual were the cause of the difficulty.

Satan persuaded Adam and Eve to sin by using the same misrepresentation of God's character as he had practiced in heaven. He made them think that God was severe and tyrannical. Then he claimed that God's unjust restrictions had led to our first parents' fall, as they had led to his own rebellion.

In banishing Satan from heaven, God declared His justice and honor. But when humanity sinned, God gave evidence of His love by offering up His Son to die for the fallen race. In the atonement we see the character of God revealed. The mighty argument of the cross demonstrates that sin was in no way the fault of God's government. During the Savior's earthly ministry, the great deceiver's character was unmasked. The daring blasphemy of his demand that Christ worship him, the unsleeping evil intent that hunted Jesus from place to place, inspiring the hearts of priests and people to reject His love and to cry, "Crucify Him! Crucify Him!"—all this drew the amazement and indignation of the universe. The prince of evil exerted all his power and crafty skills to destroy Jesus. Satan used human beings as his agents to fill the Savior's life with suffering and sorrow. And on Calvary the pent-up fires of envy and spite, hatred and revenge, burst out against the Son of God.

Now Satan's guilt stood out plainly, without excuse. He had revealed his true character. Satan's lying charges against God's character appeared as they truly were. He had accused God of seeking to exalt Himself by requiring obedience from His creatures. He had declared that while the Creator demanded self-denial from all others, He Himself practiced no self-denial and made no sacrifice. Now it was clear that the Ruler of the universe had made the greatest sacrifice that love could make, for "God was in Christ reconciling the world to Himself" (2 Corinthians 5:19). In order to destroy sin, Christ had humbled Himself and become obedient to the point of death.

An Argument in Our Behalf

All heaven saw God's justice revealed. Lucifer had claimed that the sinful race was beyond redemption. But the penalty of the law fell on Him who was equal with God. Sinners were now free to accept the righteousness of Christ and by repentance and humility triumph over Satan's power.

But Christ did not come to earth to die just so that He could redeem humanity. He came to demonstrate to all the worlds that God's law is unchangeable. The death of Christ proves that the law is permanent and demonstrates that justice and mercy are the foundation of God's government. In the final judgment it will be clear that no cause for sin exists. When the Judge of all the earth demands of Satan, "Why have you rebelled against Me?" the originator of evil will have no excuse to offer.

The Savior's dying cry, "It is finished," rang the death knell for Satan. The long-standing great controversy* was then decided, the final eradication of evil made certain. When the day comes, "'burning like an oven, . . . all the proud, yes, all who do wickedly will be stubble. And the day which is coming shall burn them up,' says the Lord of hosts, 'that will leave them neither root nor branch'" (Malachi 4:1).

Evil will never arise again. The law of God will be honored as the law of liberty. A tested and proved creation will never again turn from loyalty to Him who has demonstrated that His character is fathomless love and infinite wisdom.

---

* The "great controversy" between Christ and Satan is over God's character, His justice, and His law.

Chapter 2

HOPE FOR TRIUMPH OVER EVIL

I will put enmity between you and the woman, and between your seed and her Seed; He shall bruise your head, and you shall bruise His heel" (Genesis 3:15). This enmity, or hostility, is not natural. When Adam and Eve broke the divine law, their natures became evil, in harmony with Satan. Fallen angels and wicked people united in desperate companionship. If God had not intervened, Satan and humanity would have formed an alliance against Heaven, and the whole human family would have been united in opposition to God.

When Satan heard that enmity would exist between himself and the woman, and between his seed and her seed, he knew that by some means human beings were going to be enabled to resist his power.

Grace From Christ

Christ implants in us resistance against Satan. Without this converting grace and renewing power, we would continue as Satan's servants, always ready to obey him. But the new principle in the heart creates conflict; the power that Christ gives enables us to resist the tyrant. To hate sin instead of loving it displays a principle that is entirely from above.

The world's reception of Jesus strikingly displayed the antagonism between Christ and Satan. The purity and holiness of Christ stirred up the hatred of the ungodly against Him. His self-denial was a constant rebuke to a proud, sensual people. Satan and evil angels joined with evil human beings against the Champion of truth. They show the same enmity toward Christ's followers. Whoever resists temptation will ignite Satan's anger. Christ and Satan cannot harmonize. "All who desire to live godly in Christ Jesus will suffer persecution" (2 Timothy 3:12).

Satan's representatives try to deceive Christ's followers and draw them away from their loyalty. They twist Scripture to achieve their goal. The spirit that put Christ to death moves the wicked to destroy His followers. All this is foreshadowed in that first prophecy: "I will put enmity between you and the woman, and between your seed and her Seed."

Why is it that Satan meets no more resistance than he does? Because the soldiers of Christ have so little real connection with Christ. Sin is not repulsive to them, as it was to their Master. They do not go against it with determined resistance. They are blind to the character of the prince of darkness. So many do not know that their enemy is a mighty general, warring against Christ. Even ministers of the gospel overlook the evidences of Satan's activity. They seem to ignore the fact that he even exists.

An Alert Enemy

This alert enemy is intruding his presence into every household, every street, in the churches, in national councils, in courts of justice. He is busy perplexing, deceiving, seducing, everywhere ruining the souls and bodies of men, women, and children. He breaks up families, planting seeds of hatred, strife, rebellion, and murder. And the world seems to think that God has decreed these things and so they must exist. All who are not committed followers of Christ are servants of Satan. When Christians choose to associate with the ungodly, they expose themselves to temptation. Satan hides himself from view and draws his deceptive covering over their eyes.

Following worldly customs converts the church to the world, never the world to Christ. Familiarity with sin will cause it to seem less repulsive. When we encounter trials because we are doing what God wants, we may be sure that He will protect us. But if we place ourselves where we will be tempted, sooner or later we will fall.

The tempter often works most successfully through those whom we least suspect of being under his control. Talent and culture are gifts of God, but when these lead away from Him, they become a trap. Many people with cultured intellects and pleasant manners are polished instruments in the hands of Satan.

Never forget the inspired warning ringing down the centuries to our time: "Be sober, be vigilant; because your adversary the devil walks about like a roaring lion, seeking whom he may devour" (1 Peter 5:8). "Put on the whole armor of God, that you may be able to stand against the wiles of the devil" (Ephesians 6:11). Our great enemy is preparing for his last campaign. All who follow Jesus will have conflicts with this enemy. The more nearly Christians imitate the divine Pattern, the more surely they will make themselves a target for the attacks of Satan.

Satan attacked Christ with fierce and subtle temptations, but Jesus repulsed him in every conflict. Those victories make it possible for us to conquer. Christ will give strength to all who seek it. Satan cannot overcome any without their own consent. The tempter has no power to control the will or force the person to sin. He can cause distress, but not defilement. The fact that Christ conquered should inspire His followers with courage to fight the battle against sin and Satan.

Angels Help

Angels of God and evil spirits are plainly revealed in Scripture and are interwoven with human history. Many think that the holy angels who "minister for those who will inherit salvation" (Hebrews 1:14) are actually the spirits of the dead. But the Scriptures present proof that they are not disembodied spirits of the dead.

Before God created human beings, angels were in existence, for when the foundations of the earth were laid, "the morning stars sang together, and all the sons of God shouted for joy" (Job 38:7). After the fall of Adam and Eve but before any human being had died, God sent angels to guard the tree of life. Angels are superior to humans, for man was made "a little lower than the angels" (Psalm 8:5).

Says the prophet, "I heard the voice of many angels around the throne" (Revelation 5:11). In the presence of the King of kings they wait—"ministers of His, who do His pleasure," "heeding the voice of His word," "an innumerable company" (Psalm 103:21, 20; Hebrews 12:22). They go out as God's messengers, "in appearance like a flash of lightning," their flight is so swift (Ezekiel 1:14). The angel that appeared at the Savior's tomb, with his face "like lightning," caused the soldiers to quake with fear of him, and they "became like dead men" (Matthew 28:3, 4). When Sennacherib blasphemed God and threatened Israel, "the angel of the Lord went out, and killed in the camp of the Assyrians one hundred and eighty-five thousand" (2 Kings 19:35).

God sends angels on missions of mercy to His children. To Abraham, with promises of blessing; to Lot, to rescue him from Sodom's doom; to Elijah, about to die in the desert; to Elisha, with chariots and horses of fire when he was surrounded by his enemies; to Daniel, when he was abandoned to become the lions' prey; to Peter, doomed to death in Herod's dungeon; to the apostles in Philippi's jail; to Paul in the stormy night on the sea; to open the mind of Cornelius to receive the gospel; to send Peter with the message of salvation to the Gentile stranger—in all these ways holy angels have ministered to God's people.

Guardian Angels

God has appointed a guardian angel to every follower of Christ. "The angel of the Lord encamps all around those who fear Him, and delivers them" (Psalm 34:7). Speaking of those who believe in Him, Jesus said, "In heaven their angels always see the face of My Father" (Matthew 18:10). God's people are exposed to the unsleeping hatred of the prince of darkness, but God assures them that the angels never stop guarding them. God gives them this assurance because they will have to face mighty agencies of evil—agencies that are numerous, determined, and untiring.

Evil Angels Oppose God's Plans

Evil spirits were originally created sinless. They were equal in nature, power, and glory with the holy beings that are now God's messengers. But now they are fallen because of sin, and they have joined together to dishonor God and destroy humanity. United with Satan in rebellion, they cooperate with him in warfare against divine authority.

Old Testament history mentions their existence, but during the time when Christ was on earth evil spirits showed their power in the most striking ways. Christ had come to redeem humanity, and Satan was determined to control the world. He had succeeded in establishing idol worship in every part of the earth except Palestine. Christ came to the only land not fully yielded to the tempter, stretched out His arms of love, and invited all to find pardon and peace in Him. The angels of darkness understood that if Christ's mission were successful, their rule would end soon.

The New Testament clearly states that people have been possessed with demons. Such people were not simply suffering with disease from natural causes. Christ recognized the direct presence and influence of evil spirits. The demon-possessed men at Gadara were wretched maniacs, writhing, foaming, and raging, and they were doing violence to themselves and putting in danger everyone else who came near them. Their bleeding, disfigured bodies and deranged minds made a spectacle that pleased the prince of darkness. One of the demons controlling the sufferers said, "My name is Legion; for we are many" (Mark 5:9). In the Roman army a legion consisted of from three to five thousand men. At the command of Jesus the evil spirits fled from their victims, leaving them subdued, intelligent, and gentle. But the demons swept a herd of pigs into the sea. To the people living in Gadara, the loss outweighed the blessing Christ had brought, and so they asked the divine Healer to leave. (See Matthew 8:28-34.) By blaming Jesus for their loss, Satan stirred up the selfish fears of the people and prevented them from listening to His words.

Christ allowed the evil spirits to destroy the pigs as a rebuke to Jews who were raising unclean animals for profit. If Christ had not restrained the demons, they would have plunged not only the pigs, but also their keepers and owners, into the sea.

Furthermore, God permitted this event so that the disciples could witness the cruel power of Satan on both people and animals and would not be deceived by his delusions. Jesus also wanted the people to see His power to break Satan's hold and release his captives. Though Jesus Himself went away, the men He had so amazingly delivered remained there to tell about the mercy of their Benefactor.

The Bible records other examples: the daughter of the Syro-Phoenician woman, severely afflicted with a devil whom Jesus cast out by His word (Mark 7:25-30); a youth who had a spirit who had often "thrown him both into the fire and into the water to destroy him" (Mark 9:17-27); the maniac, tormented by a spirit of an unclean devil who disturbed the Sabbath quiet at Capernaum (Luke 4:33-36)—the Savior healed them all. In nearly every instance, Christ addressed the demon as an intelligent being, commanding him not to torment his victim ever again. The worshipers at Capernaum "were all amazed and spoke among themselves, saying, 'What a word this is! For with authority and power He commands the unclean spirits, and they come out'" (verse 36).

In order to get supernatural power, some welcomed the satanic influence. Of course, these people had no conflict with the demons. Included in this group were those who had the spirit of divination— Simon Magus, Elymas the sorcerer, and the slave girl who followed Paul and Silas at Philippi (see Acts 8:9, 18; 13:8; 16:16-18).

Danger

None are in greater danger than those who deny that the devil and his angels exist. Many accept their suggestions while they think they are following their own wisdom. As we approach the end of time, when Satan will work with his greatest power to deceive, he spreads everywhere the belief that he does not exist. It is his policy to conceal himself and his way of working.

The great deceiver is afraid that we will become acquainted with his deceptions. To disguise his real character, he has influenced people to portray him as something to ridicule or despise. He is pleased to be painted as comical, misshapen, half animal and half human. He is pleased to hear his name used in jokes and mockery. Because he has masked himself with superb skill, many people ask, "Does such a being really exist?" Because Satan can easily control the minds of those who are unaware of his influence, the Word of God reveals to us his secret forces, and this puts us on guard.

Safety With Jesus

We may find shelter and deliverance in our Redeemer's superior power. We carefully make our houses secure with bolts and locks to protect our property and lives from evil people. But seldom do we think of the evil angels and that, in our own strength, we have no defense against their attacks. If they are allowed, they can confuse our minds, torment our bodies, and destroy our possessions and our lives. But those who follow Christ are safe under His watchful care. Angels that excel in strength are sent to protect them. The wicked one cannot break through the guard that God has stationed around His people.

Chapter 3

DANGEROUS SEDUCTIONS

The great controversy between Christ and Satan will close soon, and the wicked one is increasing his efforts to defeat the work of Christ for humanity. His aim is to hold people in darkness and rebellion until the Savior's sanctuary ministry is over. When people in the church are indifferent, Satan is not concerned. But when hearts inquire, "What must I do to be saved?" he is there to match his power against Christ and to counteract the Holy Spirit's influence.

On one occasion, when the angels came to present themselves before the Lord, Satan also came among them, not to bow before the Eternal King, but to carry forward his evil plans against the righteous (see Job 1:6). He is present when Christians gather for worship, working diligently to control the minds of the worshipers. As he sees the messenger of God studying the Scriptures, he notices the subject to be presented. Then he uses his subtle skills and shrewdness so that the message may not reach those whom he is deceiving on that very point. The one who most needs the warning will be urged into some business transaction or will be prevented in some other way from hearing the word.

Satan sees the Lord's servants burdened because of the darkness that surrounds the people. He hears their prayers for divine grace and power to break the spell of indifference and laziness. Then with renewed zeal Satan tempts people to indulge their appetites or gratify themselves, and in this way he dulls their perceptions so that they fail to hear the very things they most need to learn.

Satan knows that all who neglect to pray and read the Bible will be overcome by his attacks. So he invents every possible diversion to occupy the mind. His right-hand helpers are always active when God is at work. They will describe the most earnest, self-denying servants of Christ as deceived or deceivers. Their work is to misrepresent the motives of every noble deed, to spread doubts, and arouse suspicion in the minds of the inexperienced. But we can easily see whose children they are, whose example they follow, and whose work they do. "You will know them by their fruits" (Matthew 7:16). (See also Revelation 12:10.)

The Truth Sanctifies

The great deceiver has many heresies prepared to fit the different tastes of those he wants to ruin. His plan is to bring into the church insincere, unconverted people who will encourage doubt and unbelief. Many who have no real faith in God agree to a few principles of truth and pass as Christians, and in this way they are able to introduce error as Bible doctrine. Satan knows that the truth, received in love, sanctifies the life. So he tries to substitute false theories, fables, another gospel. From the beginning, servants of God have opposed false teachers, not because they considered them vicious people, but because they taught falsehoods that were fatal to the spiritual life. Elijah, Jeremiah, Paul, firmly opposed those who were turning others from the Word of God. The liberal mind-set that thinks that correct faith is not important found no welcome with these holy defenders of truth.

The vague and inventive interpretations of Scripture and the conflicting religious theories in the Christian world are the work of our great adversary to confuse minds. The discord and division among the churches come mostly from twisting the Scriptures to support a favorite theory.

In order to prove false doctrines, some take hold of passages of Scripture separated from the context. They quote half a verse as proving their point, when the remaining portion shows that the meaning is the opposite. With the wily deceit of the serpent they take their position behind unrelated statements intended to please carnal desires. Others turn to figures and symbols, interpret them to suit their ideas with little care for the testimony of Scripture as its own interpreter, and then present their erratic thoughts as the teachings of the Bible.

The Whole Bible a Guide

Whenever people begin to study the Scriptures without a prayerful, teachable spirit, they will twist the plainest passages away from their true meaning. The whole Bible should be given to the people just as it reads.

God gave the sure word of prophecy. Angels and even Christ Himself came to make known to Daniel and John the things that "must shortly take place" (Revelation 1:1). God did not reveal important matters about our salvation in a way to perplex and mislead the person who is honestly seeking for truth. The Word of God is plain to all who study it with a prayerful heart.

By the cry "Open-mindedness" people are blinded to Satan's deceptions. He succeeds in displacing the Bible with human speculations. People set aside the law of God, and the churches are in slavery to sin while they claim to be free.

God has permitted a flood of light to pour over the world in scientific discoveries. But if the Word of God is not their guide, even the greatest minds become bewildered in trying to investigate how science and revelation fit together.

Human knowledge is partial and imperfect. This is why many are unable to harmonize their ideas of science with Scripture. Many accept as scientific facts things that are only theories, and they think that they should test God's Word by "what is falsely called knowledge" (1 Timothy 6:20). Because they cannot explain the Creator and His works by natural laws, they consider Bible history as unreliable. Those who doubt the Old and New Testaments too often go a step further and doubt the existence of God. Once they let go of their anchor, they beat about on the rocks of unbelief.

It is a masterpiece of Satan's deceptions to keep people speculating about things that God has not made known. Lucifer became dissatisfied because God did not share with him all the secrets of God's purposes, and he turned his back on the things God had revealed. Now he tries to fill people with the same spirit and lead them also to ignore the direct commands of God.

Truth Rejected Because It Involves a Cross

The less spiritual and self-denying the doctrines presented, the greater the favor with which people receive them. Satan is ready to supply what people want, and he palms off deception in the place of truth. This is how the papacy gained its power over the minds of so many.

And by rejecting the truth because it involves a cross, Protestants are following the same path. All who study convenience and popular opinion, so that they will not be out of step with the world, will be left to receive "destructive heresies" in place of truth (2 Peter 2:1). Those who look with horror on one deception will eagerly receive another.*

Dangerous Errors

The lying wonders of spiritualism are among Satan's most successful agencies. When people reject the truth, they become easy targets for deception.

Another error is the doctrine that denies the deity of Christ, claiming that He had no existence before He was born into this world. This theory contradicts Jesus' own statements about His relationship with the Father and His pre-existence. It undermines faith in the Bible as a revelation from God. If people reject the testimony of Scripture about the deity of Christ, it is useless to argue with them. No argument, however strong, could convince them. None who

---

* In the complete book, *The Great Controversy*, readers will find the story of how most of the Christian world gradually departed from the teachings of the Bible.

hold this error can have a true understanding of Christ or of God's plan for our redemption.

Still another error is the belief that Satan does not exist as a personal being, that the Bible uses that name simply to represent people's evil thoughts and desires.

Some teach that the second advent of Christ is His coming to each individual at death. This is a deception to divert minds from Jesus' personal coming in the clouds of heaven. By this means, Satan has been saying, "Behold, he is in the secret chambers" (see Matthew 24:23-26, KJV), and many have been lost by accepting this deception.

Again, many scientists claim that there can be no real answer to prayer, because this would be a violation of law—a miracle, and miracles have no existence. The universe, they say, is governed by fixed laws, and God Himself does nothing against these laws. So they represent God as limited by His own laws—as if divine laws could exclude divine freedom.

Did not Christ and His apostles work miracles? The same Savior is as willing to listen to the prayer of faith today as when He walked visibly on the earth. The natural cooperates with the supernatural. It is a part of God's plan to grant us, in answer to the prayer of faith, what He would not give if we did not ask in faith.

The Landmarks of the Word

False doctrines among the churches remove landmarks that the Word of God has established. Few people stop when they have rejected just one truth. The majority set aside one after another of the principles of truth, until they reject the Christian faith altogether.

The errors of popular theology have driven many people to skepticism. It is impossible for them to accept doctrines that outrage their sense of justice, mercy, and kindness. Since the churches say that these are the teachings of the Bible, such people refuse to acknowledge it as the Word of God.

Many people look distrustfully at the Word of God because it rebukes and condemns sin. Those who are unwilling to obey try to overthrow its authority. Many reject religion in order to justify their neglect of duty. Others, who love ease too much to accomplish anything that requires self-denial, acquire a reputation for superior wisdom by criticizing the Bible.

Many feel it is a virtue to stand on the side of unbelief, skepticism, and irreligion. But underneath an appearance of honesty they act from self-confidence and pride. Many delight in finding something in the Scriptures to puzzle the minds of others. Some at first reason on the wrong side just because they love a controversy. But once they have openly expressed unbelief, they then join with the ungodly.

Enough Evidence

In His Word God has given enough evidence of its divine character. Yet finite minds are inadequate to comprehend fully the intentions of the Infinite One. "How unsearchable are His judgments and His ways past finding out!" (Romans 11:33). We can understand His actions and motives enough to see unlimited love and mercy united to infinite power. Our Father in heaven will reveal to us as much as it is good for us to know. Beyond that we must trust the Hand that is all-powerful, the Heart that is full of love.

God will never remove all excuse for unbelief. All who look for hooks to hang their doubts on will find them. And those who refuse to obey until every objection is gone will never come to the light. The unrenewed heart is in conflict with God. But faith is inspired by the Holy Spirit and will flourish as we cherish it. No one can become strong in faith without persistent effort. If people allow themselves to raise trivial objections, they will find doubt becoming stronger.

But those who doubt and distrust the assurance of His grace dishonor Christ. They are unproductive trees that block the sunlight from other plants, causing them to droop and die under their chilling shadow. The lifework of these people will always stand as a witness against them.

For those who honestly want to be freed from doubts, there is only one course to pursue. Instead of questioning the things they do not understand, they should pay attention to the light that already shines on them, and they will receive greater light.

Satan can produce a counterfeit that so closely resembles the truth that it deceives those who are willing to be deceived, who want to avoid the sacrifice that the truth demands. But it is impossible for him to hold even one person under his power who honestly desires to know the truth, no matter what the cost. Christ is the truth, the "Light which gives light to every man coming into the world" (John 1:9). "If anyone wills to do His will, he shall know concerning the doctrine" (John 7:17). The Lord permits His people to go through the fiery ordeal of temptation, not because He enjoys their distress, but because this is essential to their final victory. It would be inconsistent with His own glory to shield them from temptation, because the purpose of the trial is to prepare them to resist all the attractions of evil. Neither wicked people nor devils can shut God's presence away from His people if they will confess their sins, put them away, and claim His promises. Every temptation, open or secret, they may successfully resist, "'not by might nor by power, but by My Spirit,' says the Lord of hosts" (Zechariah 4:6).

"Who is he who will harm you if you become followers of what is good?" (1 Peter 3:13). Satan is well aware that the weakest Christian who abides in Christ is more than a match for all the armies of darkness. For this reason, he tries to draw the soldiers of the cross away from their strong defenses, while he waits in ambush, ready to destroy all who step onto his ground. Only when we rely on God and obey all His commandments can we be secure.

No one is safe for a day or an hour without prayer. Plead with the Lord for wisdom to understand His Word. Satan is an expert in quoting Scripture, placing his own interpretation on passages in hopes of causing us to stumble. We should study with humility of heart. While we must constantly guard against Satan's deceptions, we should pray in faith continually, "Do not lead us into temptation" (Matthew 6:13).

Chapter 4

EVERLASTING LIFE

Satan, who had stirred up rebellion in heaven, wanted to bring those living on the earth to join him in his warfare against God. Adam and Eve had been perfectly happy in obeying God's law—a constant testimony against the claim Satan had made in heaven that God's law was oppressive. Satan was determined to cause their fall so that he could possess the earth and establish his kingdom here in opposition to the Most High.

God had warned Adam and Eve about this dangerous enemy, but Satan worked in the dark, hiding his intentions. Using the snake as his medium, whose appearance then was fascinating, he said to Eve, "Has God indeed said, 'You shall not eat of every tree of the garden'?" Eve dared to talk with him and became a victim of his deceptive skill: "The woman said to the serpent, 'We may eat of the fruit of the trees of the garden; but of the fruit of the tree which is in the midst of the garden, God has said, "You shall not eat it, nor shall you touch it, lest you die."' Then the serpent said to the woman, 'You will not surely die. For God knows that in the day you eat of it your eyes will be opened, and you will be like God, knowing good and evil'" (Genesis 3:1-5).

Eve yielded to temptation, and through her influence Adam sinned. They accepted the words of the serpent. They distrusted their Creator and imagined that He was restricting their liberty.

But what did Adam find to be the meaning of the words, "In the day that you eat of it you shall surely die"? Was he going to be ushered into a higher existence? Adam did not find this to be the meaning of the divine sentence. God declared that as a penalty for his sin, he and his descendants would return to the ground: "Dust you are, and to dust you shall return" (Genesis 3:19). Satan's words, "Your eyes will be opened," proved to be true only in this sense: their eyes were opened to see how foolish they had been. They did know evil, and they tasted the bitter fruit of transgression.

The fruit of the tree of life had the power to sustain life forever. Adam would have continued to enjoy free access to this tree and would never have died, but when he sinned he was cut off from the tree of life and became subject to death. He had lost immortality by his sin. There could have been no hope for the fallen race if God had not brought immortality within their reach by the sacrifice of His Son. While "death spread to all men, because all sinned" (Romans 5:12), Christ has "brought life and immortality to light through the gospel" (2 Timothy 1:10). We can receive immortality only through Christ. "He who believes in the Son has everlasting life; and he who does not believe the Son shall not see life." (John 3:36).

The Great Lie

The one who promised Adam life in disobedience was the great deceiver. And the serpent's claim in Eden—"You will not surely die"—was the first sermon ever preached on the immortality of the soul. Yet this claim, resting only on Satan's authority, echoes from pulpits today, and most people accept it as readily as our first parents did. The divine sentence, "The soul who sins shall die" (Ezekiel 18:20), is made to mean, The soul who sins shall *not* die, but live eternally. If God had allowed Adam and Eve free access to the tree of life after their fall, sin would have been immortalized. But God has not permitted even one of the family of Adam to eat of the life-giving fruit. As a result, there is no immortal sinner.

After the Fall, Satan instructed his angels to instill in people the belief that they are naturally immortal. After persuading the people to accept this error, evil angels were to lead them to conclude that sinners would live in eternal misery. Now the prince of darkness presents God as a revengeful tyrant who plunges into hell all who do not please Him, and looks down on them with satisfaction while they writhe in eternal flames. In this way the one who started all evil paints the Benefactor of the human race with his own characteristics. Cruelty is satanic. God is love. Satan is the enemy who tempts us to sin and then destroys us if he can. How offensive to love, mercy, and justice it is to teach that God torments the wicked dead in an eternally burning hell, that for the sins of a brief life on earth they suffer torture as long as God shall live! A well-educated minister said, "The sight of hell's torments will [increase] the happiness of the saints forever. . . . It will make them [conscious] of how happy they are."

Where can anyone find such teaching in God's Word? Will the redeemed exchange feelings of common humanity for the cruelty of the savage? No, such things are not the teaching of the Book of God. "'As I live,' says the Lord God, 'I have no pleasure in the death of the wicked, but that the wicked turn from his way and live. Turn, turn from your evil ways! For why should you die?'" (Ezekiel 33:11).

Does God delight in witnessing unending tortures? Is He pleased with the groans and shrieks of suffering creatures whom He holds in the flames? Can these horrid sounds be music to the ear of Infinite Love? What a terrible blasphemy! God's glory is not increased by keeping sin alive through ages without end.

The Heresy of Eternal Torment

Untold evil has come from the heresy of eternal torment. It takes the religion of the Bible, so full of love and goodness, darkens it by superstition, and clothes it with terror. Satan has painted the character of God in false colors, making people fear, dread, and even hate our merciful Creator. The repulsive views of God that have spread over the world from the teachings of the pulpit have made millions of people skeptics and unbelievers.

Eternal torment is one of the false doctrines, the wine of abomination (Revelation 14:8; 17:2), which Babylon makes all nations drink. Ministers of Christ accepted this heresy from Rome, just as they received the false sabbath.* If we turn from God's Word and accept false doctrines because our ancestors taught them, we come under the condemnation that the Bible pronounces on Babylon. We are drinking from the wine of her abomination.

Many people are driven to the opposite error. They see that Scripture presents God as a being of love and compassion, and they cannot believe that He will condemn His creatures to an eternally burning hell. Since they hold the idea that the soul is naturally immortal, they conclude that all humanity will be saved. So the sinner can live in selfish pleasure, ignoring God's requirements, and still be welcomed into His favor. Such a doctrine, which presumes on God's mercy but ignores His justice, pleases the unconverted heart.

Universal Salvation Is Not Biblical

Believers in universal salvation twist the Scriptures. The professed minister of Christ repeats the lie that the serpent spoke in Eden, "You will not surely die." "In the day you eat of it your eyes will be opened, and you will be like God, knowing good and evil." He asserts that the worst of sinners—the murderer, the thief, the adulterer—will enter into immortal bliss after death. This is no more than a pleasing fable, designed to appeal to the unconverted heart!

If it were true that everyone went directly to heaven at death, we might well desire death rather than life. This belief has led many to commit suicide. When they are overwhelmed with trouble and disappointment, it seems easy to break the thread of life and soar into the bliss of the eternal world.

In His Word God has given decisive evidence that He will punish those who trample on His law. Is He too merciful to execute justice on the sinner? Look to the cross of Calvary. The death of God's Son testifies that "the wages of sin is death" (Romans 6:23), that every violation of God's law must receive its punishment. Christ the sinless

---

* For more information about the Sabbath, see chapter 8 of this book.

became sin for us. He bore the guilt of sin and the hiding of His Father's face until His heart was broken and His life crushed out—all this so that sinners could be redeemed. And all who refuse to accept the atonement provided at such a cost must bear their own guilt and the punishment for their own sins.

Conditions Are Specified

"I will give of the fountain of the water of life freely to him who thirsts" (Revelation 21:6). This promise is only for those who are thirsty. "He who overcomes shall inherit all things, and I will be his God and he shall be My son" (verse 7). This text also specifies conditions. To inherit all things, we must overcome sin.

"It will not be well with the wicked" (Ecclesiastes 8:13). Sinners are treasuring up for themselves "wrath in the day of wrath and revelation of the righteous judgment of God, who 'will render to each one according to his deeds'" "tribulation and anguish, on every soul of man who does evil" (Romans 2:5, 6, 9).

"No fornicator, unclean person, nor covetous man, who is an idolater, has any inheritance in the kingdom of Christ and God" (Ephesians 5:5). "Blessed are those who do His commandments, that they may have the right to the tree of life, and may enter through the gates into the city. But outside are dogs and sorcerers and sexually immoral and murderers and idolaters, and whoever loves and practices a lie" (Revelation 22:14, 15).

God has given us a clear statement of how He will deal with sin. "All the wicked He will destroy" (Psalm 145:20). "The transgressors shall be destroyed together; the future of the wicked shall be cut off" (Psalm 37:38). The authority of the divine government will put down rebellion, yet His justice in punishing sin will be consistent with the character of God as a merciful, kind being.

God does not force the will. He takes no pleasure in slavelike obedience. He wants the creatures He has made to love Him because He is worthy of love. He would like them to obey Him because they have an intelligent appreciation of His wisdom, justice, and kindness. The principles of God's government are in harmony with the Savior's command, "Love your enemies" (Matthew 5:44). God executes justice on the wicked for the good of the universe and even for the good of those who receive His judgments. He would make them happy if He could. He surrounds them with evidences of His love and follows them with offers of mercy. But they despise His love, overturn His law, and reject His mercy. Even while they constantly receive His gifts, they dishonor the Giver. The Lord is very patient with their determined self-will, but will He chain these rebels to His side and force them to do what He wants?

Not Prepared to Enter Heaven

Those who have chosen Satan as their leader are not prepared to enter the presence of God. Pride, deception, immorality, cruelty, have become established in their characters. Can they enter heaven to live forever with those whom they hated on earth? Truth will never be agreeable to a liar. Meekness will not satisfy self-esteem. Purity is not acceptable to the corrupt. Unselfish love does not appear attractive to the selfish. What enjoyment could heaven offer those who are focused on selfish interests?

Will those whose hearts are filled with hatred of God, of truth and holiness, be able to mingle with the inhabitants of heaven and join their songs of praise? God granted them years of grace to prepare for eternity with Him, but they never trained the mind to love purity. They never learned the language of heaven. Now it is too late.

A life of rebellion against God has made them unfit for heaven. Its purity and peace would be torture to them; the glory of God would be a consuming fire. They would long to escape from that holy place and would welcome destruction, just to be hidden from the face of Him who died to redeem them. It is their own choice that decides the destiny of the wicked. They voluntarily exclude themselves from heaven, and God is just and merciful in ratifying their choice. Like the waters of the Flood, the fires of the great day declare God's verdict that the wicked are incurable. They have exercised their will in revolt. When life is over, it is too late to turn their thoughts from lawbreaking to obedience, from hatred to love.

Two Destinies

"The wages of sin is death, but the gift of God is eternal life in Christ Jesus our Lord" (Romans 6:23). Life is the inheritance of the righteous, and death is the destiny of the wicked. The Bible places "the second death" in contrast with everlasting life (see Revelation 20:14).

Because of Adam's sin, death came upon the whole human race. Everyone goes down into the grave. And through the plan of salvation, all will be brought up from their graves: "There will be a resurrection of the dead, both of the just and the unjust," "for as in Adam all die, even so in Christ all shall be made alive" (Acts 24:15; 1 Corinthians 15:22).

But the Bible makes a distinction between the two classes that are resurrected: "All who are in the graves will hear His voice and come forth—those who have done good, to the resurrection of life, and those who have done evil, to the resurrection of condemnation" (John 5:28, 29).

The End of Suffering

They who have been "counted worthy" (Luke 20:35) of the resurrection of life are "blessed and holy." "Over such the second death has no power" (Revelation 20:6). But those who have not received pardon through repentance and faith must receive "the wages of sin," punishment "according to their works," which ends in the "second death."

Since it is impossible for God to save sinners in their sins, He deprives them of their existence, which their transgressions have forfeited and of which they have proven themselves unworthy. "Yet a little while and the wicked shall be no more; indeed, you will look carefully for his place, but it shall be no more" (Psalm 37:10). "They shall be as though they had never been" (Obadiah 16). They sink into hopeless, eternal oblivion.

And so God will make an end of sin. "You have destroyed the wicked; You have blotted out their name forever and ever. O enemy, destructions are finished forever!" (Psalm 9:5, 6). In the book of Revelation, John hears a universal anthem of praise without one note of discord. No lost souls blaspheme God as they writhe in never-ending torment. No wretched beings in hell will mingle their shrieks with the songs of the saved.

The error of natural immortality is the basis for the doctrine of consciousness in death. Like eternal torment, this doctrine is opposed to Scripture, to reason, and to our feelings of humanity.

According to popular belief, the redeemed in heaven know everything that takes place on earth. But how could the dead be happy in knowing the troubles of the living, in seeing them endure the sorrows, disappointments, and anguish of life? And how revolting is the belief that as soon as the breath leaves the body, the soul of the unrepentant is sent to the flames of hell!

What do the Scriptures say? Humanity is not conscious in death: "When their breath departs, they return to the earth; on that very day their plans perish" (Psalm 146:4). "The living know that they will die; but the dead know nothing. . . . Their love, their hatred, and their envy have now perished; nevermore will they have a share in anything done under the sun" (Ecclesiastes 9:5, 6). "Sheol [the grave] cannot thank You, death cannot praise You; those who go down to the pit cannot hope for Your truth. The living, the living man, he shall praise You, as I do this day" (Isaiah 38:18, 19). "In death there is no remembrance of You; in the grave who will give You thanks?" (Psalm 6:5).

On the day of Pentecost Peter declared that David "is both dead and buried, and his tomb is with us to this day. . . . For David did not ascend into the heavens" (Acts 2:29-34). The fact that David remains in the grave until the resurrection proves that the righteous do not go to heaven when they die.

Resurrection to Eternal Life

When He was about to leave His disciples, Jesus did not tell them that they would soon come to Him. "I go to prepare a place for you," He said. "And if I go and prepare a place for you, I will come again and receive you to Myself" (John 14:2, 3). Paul tells us further that "the Lord Himself will descend from heaven with a shout, with the voice of an archangel, and with the trumpet of God. And the dead in Christ will rise first. Then we who are alive and remain shall be caught up together with them in the clouds to meet the Lord in the air. And thus we shall always be with the Lord." And he adds, "Comfort one another with these words" (1 Thessalonians 4:16-18). When the Lord comes, He will break the chains of death and will raise the "dead in Christ" to eternal life.

God will judge everyone by the things written in the books and reward them as their works have been. This judgment does not take place at death. "He has appointed a day on which He will judge the world in righteousness" (Acts 17:31)."Behold, the Lord comes with ten thousands of His saints, to execute judgment on all" (Jude 14, 15).

But if the dead are already enjoying heaven or writhing in the flames of hell, what need is there for a future judgment? Ordinary minds can understand God's Word on these points. But what unbiased mind can see either wisdom or justice in the current theory? Will the righteous receive God's approving words, "Well done, good and faithful servant. . . . Enter into the joy of your lord" (Matthew 25:21), when they have already been living in His presence for long ages? Are the wicked called from torment to receive the Judge's sentence, "Depart from Me, you cursed, into . . . everlasting fire" (verse 41)?

The theory that the soul is immortal was one of those false doctrines that Rome borrowed from paganism. Martin Luther classed it with the "monstrous fables that form part of the Roman dunghill of [decrees]."* The Bible teaches that the dead sleep until the resurrection.

Immortality When Jesus Returns

Sweet rest for the weary righteous! Time, whether it is long or short, is only a moment to them. They sleep, and then the trumpet of God awakens them to a glorious immortality. "For the trumpet will sound, and the dead will be raised incorruptible. . . . So when this corruptible has put on incorruption, and this mortal has put on immortality, then shall be brought to pass the saying that is written: 'Death is swallowed up in victory'" (1 Corinthians 15:52-54).

Called to arise from their sleep, they begin to think just where they had stopped. The last sensation was the stroke of death; the last thought, that they were falling beneath the power of the grave. When they come out from the tomb, their first glad thought will be echoed in the triumphant shout, "O Death, where is your sting? O Hades, where is your victory?" (verse 55).

------

* E. Petavel, *The Problem of Immortality,* p. 255.

Chapter 5

FALSE HOPE

The doctrine that we are naturally immortal came from pagan philosophy. In the darkness of the great apostasy it became a part of the Christian faith, where it has now replaced the truth that "the dead know nothing" (Ecclesiastes 9:5). Many people believe that the spirits of the dead are the "ministering spirits sent forth to minister for those who will inherit salvation" (Hebrews 1:14).

The belief that spirits of the dead return to help the living has prepared the way for modern spiritualism. If the dead are entrusted with knowledge far beyond what they had before, why not return to earth and instruct the living? If spirits of the dead hover around their friends on earth, why not communicate with them? How can those who believe in human consciousness in death reject "divine light" that comes through glorified spirits? Here is a channel that people think is sacred but which Satan uses. Fallen angels appear as messengers from the spirit world.

The prince of evil has power to bring before people the appearance of departed friends. The counterfeit is perfect, reproduced with amazing exactness. Many take comfort in the assurance that their loved ones are enjoying heaven. Without suspecting danger, they open their lives "to deceiving spirits and doctrines of demons" (1 Timothy 4:1).

Those who went into the grave unprepared claim to be happy and to occupy high positions in heaven. Pretended visitors from the world of spirits sometimes give warnings that prove to be correct. Then, as they win people's confidence, they present doctrines that undermine the Scriptures. The fact that they speak some truths and at times foretell future events makes them appear reliable, and people accept their false teachings. The law of God is set aside, the Spirit of grace despised. The spirits deny the deity of Christ and place the Creator on a level with themselves.

While it is true that the results of trickery have often been presented as genuine manifestations, there have also been clear exhibitions of supernatural power, the direct work of evil angels. Many believe that spiritualism is nothing more than human fraud. When they come face to face with happenings that they cannot explain as anything but supernatural, they will be deceived and will accept them as the great power of God.

With help from Satan, Pharaoh's magicians counterfeited the work of God (see Exodus 7:10-12). Paul testifies that before the coming of the Lord we will see "the working of Satan, with all power, signs, and lying wonders, and with all unrighteous deception" (2 Thessalonians 2:9, 10). And John declares: "He performs great signs, so that he even makes fire come down from heaven on the earth in the sight of men. And he deceives those who dwell on the earth by those signs which he was granted to do" (Revelation 13:13, 14). This is not predicting mere tricks. People are deceived by the miracles that Satan's agents actually do, not that they only pretend to do.

Satan's Appeal to Intellectuals

To cultured and refined people, the prince of darkness presents the more refined and intellectual aspects of spiritualism. He delights the imagination with entrancing scenes and eloquent portrayals of love and charity. He leads people to take such great pride in their own wisdom that in their hearts they despise the Eternal One.

Satan deceives people now as he deceived Eve in Eden, by stirring up their ambition to exalt themselves. "You will be like God," he says, "knowing good and evil" (Genesis 3:5). Spiritualism teaches "that a human being is the creature of progression . . . toward the Godhead." It claims, "The judgment will be right, because it is the judgment of self. . . . The throne is within you." "Any just and perfect being is Christ."

In this way Satan has substituted a person's own sinful human nature for the law of God as the only rule of judgment. This is progress, not upward, but downward. Men and women will never rise higher than their standard of purity or goodness. If self is their highest ideal, they will never reach anything higher. The grace of God alone has power to exalt them. If they are left to themselves, their path will be downward.

Appeal to the Pleasure-loving

To people who are self-indulgent, pleasure-loving, and sensual, spiritualism appears in a less subtle disguise. In its grosser forms they find what agrees with their inclinations. Satan notes the sins each individual is inclined to commit and then makes sure that opportunities come along to gratify the tendency. He tempts people through intemperance, leading them to weaken their physical, mental, and moral power. He destroys thousands through indulgence of passion, brutalizing the entire nature. And to complete his work, the spirits declare that "true knowledge places a person above all law," that "whatever is, is right," that "God does not condemn," and that "*all* sins . . . are innocent." When people believe that desire is the highest law, that liberty is license, that they are accountable only to themselves, who can be surprised that corruption flourishes everywhere? Great numbers of people eagerly accept the urgings of lust. Satan sweeps into his net thousands who profess to follow Christ.

But God has given enough light to detect the snare. The very foundation of spiritualism is at war with Scripture. The Bible declares that the dead know nothing, that their thoughts have perished. They have no part in the joys or sorrows of those on earth.

Forbidden Fellowship

Furthermore, God has forbidden all pretended communication with departed spirits. The Bible says that "familiar spirits," as these visitors from other worlds were called, are "the spirits of demons" (see Numbers 25:1-3; Psalm 106:28; 1 Corinthians 10:20; Revelation

16:14). God prohibited dealing with them under penalty of death (Leviticus 19:31; 20:27). But spiritualism has made its way into scientific circles, invaded churches, and found a welcome in legislative bodies, even in the courts of kings. This mammoth deception is a revival in a new disguise of the witchcraft condemned long ago.

By representing the most evil of sinners as in heaven, Satan says to the world: "No matter whether you believe or disbelieve God and the Bible, live as you please. Heaven is your home." But the Word of God says, "Woe to those who call evil good, and good evil; who put darkness for light, and light for darkness" (Isaiah 5:20).

Bible Represented as Fiction

Lying spirits impersonate the apostles, making them contradict what they wrote when on earth. Satan is making the world believe that the Bible is fiction, a book suited to the infancy of the race but obsolete today. The Book that is to judge him and his followers he puts in the shadows. The Savior of the world he makes to be no more than a common man. And believers in spirit appearances try to make it seem that there is nothing miraculous in our Savior's life. They declare that their own miracles are far greater than the works of Christ.

Spiritualism is now adopting a Christian appearance. But it cannot deny or hide its teachings. In its present form it is a more dangerous and more subtle deception. It now professes to accept Christ and the Bible, but it interprets the Bible in a way that is pleasing to the unrenewed heart. It dwells on love as the chief attribute of God, but it degrades this love to a weak sentimentalism. God's condemnations of sin, the requirements of His holy law, are kept out of sight. Fables lead men and women to reject the Bible as the foundation of their faith. Christ is denied as surely as before, but most people do not recognize the deception.

Few have a proper understanding of spiritualism's deceptive power. Many tamper with it merely out of curiosity. They would be horrified at the thought of yielding to the spirits' control. But they dare to go onto forbidden ground, and the destroyer exercises his power on them against their will. If he can get them to submit their minds to his direction just once, he will hold them captive. Nothing but the power of God, in answer to earnest prayer, can deliver them.

All who willfully cherish known sin are inviting Satan's temptations. They separate themselves from God and the watchcare of His angels, leaving themselves without defense.

"When they say to you, 'Seek those who are mediums and wizards, who whisper and mutter,' should not a people seek their God? Should they seek the dead on behalf of the living? To the law and to the testimony! If they do not speak according to this word, it is because there is no light in them" (Isaiah 8:19, 20).

If people had been willing to accept the Bible truth concerning our human nature and the condition of the dead, they would see in spiritualism Satan's power and lying wonders. But so many close their eyes to the light, and Satan weaves his snares around them. "Because they did not receive the love of the truth, that they might be saved," therefore "God will send them strong delusion, that they should believe the lie" (2 Thessalonians 2:10, 11).

Those who oppose spiritualism attack Satan and his angels. Satan will not yield one inch of ground except as the heavenly messengers drive him back. He can quote Scripture and will twist its teachings. Those who intend to stand in this time of danger must understand for themselves what the Bible teaches.

Understanding the Scriptures

Spirits of devils impersonating relatives or friends will appeal to our tender sympathies and will work miracles. We must resist them with the Bible truth that the dead know nothing and that they who appear this way are the spirits of devils.

All whose faith is not established on the Word of God will be deceived and overcome. Satan works "with all unrighteous deception," and his deceptions will increase. But those who are looking for a knowledge of the truth and who purify their lives through obedience will find a sure defense in the God of truth. The Savior would sooner send every angel out of heaven to protect His people than leave one person who trusts in Him to be overcome by Satan. Those who comfort themselves with the assurance that there is no punishment for the sinner, who reject the truths that Heaven has provided as a defense for the day of trouble, will accept the lies that Satan offers, the deceptive claims of spiritualism.

Scoffers ridicule what Scripture says about the plan of salvation and the punishment that will fall on those who reject truth. They pretend to have great pity for minds so narrow, weak, and superstitious as to obey the requirements of God's law. They have yielded themselves to the tempter so fully, united with him so closely, and drunk so deeply of his spirit that they have no desire to break away from his snare.

Satan laid the foundation of his work in the assurance he gave to Eve in Eden: "You will not surely die" (Genesis 3:4). "In the day you eat of it your eyes will be opened, and you will be like God, knowing good and evil" (verse 5). He will reach his masterpiece of deception at the very end of time. Says the prophet: "I saw three unclean spirits like frogs. . . . For they are the spirits of demons, performing signs, which go out to the kings of the earth and of the whole world, to gather them to the battle of that great day of God Almighty" (Revelation 16:13, 14).

Except for those whom God's power keeps through faith in His Word, the whole world will be swept into the ranks of this deception. The people are quickly being lulled into a fatal security, and only the outpouring of God's wrath will awaken them.

Chapter 6

TRUE PEACE

Wherever the Word of God has been faithfully preached, the results that followed demonstrated that it was from God. Sinners felt their consciences awaken. Deep conviction took hold of their minds and hearts. They had a sense of God's righteousness, and they cried out, "Who will deliver me from this body of death?" (Romans 7:24). As the cross of Jesus was revealed, they saw that nothing but the merits of Christ could atone for their sins. Through the blood of Jesus, "God had passed over the sins that were previously committed" (Romans 3:25).

These people believed and were baptized and rose to walk in newness of life. By the faith of the Son of God they would follow in His steps, reflect His character, and purify themselves even as He is pure. Things they once hated they now loved, and things they once loved they hated. The proud became meek, the vain and haughty became serious and inconspicuous. The drunken became sober, the immoral pure. Christians did not seek the outward decoration of "arranging the hair, of wearing gold, or of putting on fine apparel," but "the incorruptible beauty of a gentle and quiet spirit, which is very precious in the sight of God" (1 Peter 3:3, 4).

Revivals brought solemn appeals to the sinner. They bore fruit in people who did not draw back from self-denial but rejoiced that they were counted worthy to suffer for the sake of Christ. Onlookers could see a transformation in those who decided to follow Jesus. Effects like these used to follow times of religious awakening.

But many modern revivals are very different from these. It is true that many people claim to be converted, and large numbers join the churches. But the results do not support the belief that there has been an increase of real spiritual life in those who responded. The light that flames up for a while soon dies out.

Popular revivals too often excite the emotions, appealing to the love for something new and startling. People converted in this way have little desire to listen to Bible truth. Unless a religious service has something sensational in it, it does not attract them.

With every truly converted person, relating to God and to eternal things will be the great topic of life. Where in the popular churches of today is the spirit of consecration to God? Converts do not turn their backs on pride and love of the world. They are no more willing to deny self and follow the meek and lowly Jesus than they were before their conversion. Godliness has almost completely gone away from many of the churches.

True Followers of Christ

Despite the widespread decline in faith, there are true followers of Christ in these churches. Before God finally brings His judgments, among the people of the Lord there will be a revival of authentic godliness not seen since the time of the apostles. The Spirit of God will be poured out. Many will separate from those churches in which love of this world has replaced love for God and His Word. Many ministers and people will gladly accept the great truths that prepare a people for the Lord's second coming.

Satan wants to interfere with this work, and before the time for such a movement arrives, he will try to prevent it by bringing in a counterfeit. In churches that he can bring under his power, he will make it appear that God is pouring out His special blessing. Many will boast, "God is working marvelously," when the work belongs to another spirit. Under a religious disguise, Satan will try to extend his influence over the Christian world. In such revivals there is an emotional excitement, a mingling of the true with the false, well designed to mislead.

Yet in the light of God's Word it is not difficult to recognize the nature of these movements. Wherever people neglect the instruction of the Bible, turning away from those plain, heart-testing truths that require them to deny self and renounce the world, there we may be sure that God is not bestowing His blessing. And by the rule "You will know them by their fruits" (Matthew 7:16), it is clear that these movements are not the work of the Spirit of God.

The truths of God's Word are a shield against Satan's deceptions. Neglecting these truths has opened the door to the evils that are now widespread in the world. To a great extent people have lost sight of the importance of God's law. A wrong idea about the divine law has led to errors in conversion and sanctification, lowering the standard of godly living. Here we find the reason the Spirit of God is missing in the revivals of today.

The Law of Liberty

Many religious teachers claim that Christ abolished the law by His death. Some say it is a heavy yoke, and in contrast to the "bondage" of the law they present the "liberty" that the gospel supposedly grants us to enjoy.

But this is not the way the prophets and apostles thought of the holy law of God. David said, "I will walk at liberty, for I seek Your precepts" (Psalm 119:45). The apostle James refers to the Ten Commandments as "the perfect law of liberty" (James 1:25). John the revelator pronounces a blessing on those "who do His commandments, that they may have the right to the tree of life, and may enter through the gates into the city" (Revelation 22:14).

If it had been possible to change the law or set it aside, Christ would not have needed to die to save us from the penalty of sin. The Son of God came to "exalt the law and make it honorable" (Isaiah 42:21). He said, "Do not think that I came to destroy the Law"; "till heaven and earth pass away, one jot or one tittle shall by no means pass from the law" (Matthew 5:17, 18). Concerning Himself Jesus declared, "I delight to do Your will, O my God, and Your law is within my heart" (Psalm 40:8).

The law of God is unchangeable, a revelation of its Author's character. God is love, and His law is love. "Love is the fulfillment of the law" (Romans 13:10). The psalmist says, "Your law is truth"; "all Your commandments are righteousness (Psalm 119:142, 172). Paul declares, "The law is holy, and the commandment holy and just and good" (Romans 7:12). A law like this must be as long-lasting as its Author.

It is the work of conversion and sanctification to restore people to God by leading them to obey the principles of His law. In the beginning, human beings were in perfect harmony with the law of God. But sin alienated them from their Maker. Their hearts were at war with God's law. "The carnal mind is enmity against God; for it is not subject to the law of God, nor indeed can be" (Romans 8:7). But "God so loved the world that He gave His only begotten Son" (John 3:16), so that sinners could be reconciled to God and be brought again into harmony with their Maker. This change is the new birth, without which the sinner "cannot see the kingdom of God" (verse 3).

Conviction of Sin

The first step in becoming right with God is the conviction of sin. "Sin is lawlessness" (1 John 3:4). "By the law is the knowledge of sin" (Romans 3:20). In order to see their guilt, sinners must test their character by God's law—a mirror that shows what a perfect righteous character looks like and enables them to recognize the defects in their own.

The law shows us our sin, but it provides no remedy. It declares that death is the reward of the transgressor. Only the gospel of Christ can free us from the condemnation or the defilement of sin. We must have repentance toward God, whose law we have broken, and faith in Christ, our atoning sacrifice. In this way we receive forgiveness for "sins that were previously committed" (Romans 3:25) and become children of God.

Luther Illustrates Finding Forgiveness and Salvation

A desire to find peace with God led Martin Luther to devote himself to a monk's life. As part of this, he was required to do the lowest jobs and to beg from house to house. He patiently endured this humiliation, believing it was necessary because of his sins.

He led a very strict life, trying to subdue the evils of his nature by fasting, vigils, and whippings. Later he said, "If ever monk could gain heaven by his monkish works, I should certainly have been entitled to it. . . . If it had continued much longer, I should have carried my [self-denial] even to death."* With all his efforts, his burdened heart found no relief. Finally he was driven nearly to despair.

When it seemed that all hope was gone, God raised up a friend for him. Staupitz opened the Word of God to Luther's mind and urged him to look away from self and look to Jesus. "Instead of torturing yourself on account of your sins, throw yourself into the Redeemer's arms. Trust in Him, in the righteousness of His life, in the atonement of His death. . . . The Son of God . . . became man to give you the assurance of God's favor. . . . Love Him who first loved you."† His words made a deep impression on Luther's mind. Peace came to his troubled heart.

Later Luther spoke from the pulpit in solemn warning. He told the people how offensive sin is to God and how impossible it is for any of us by our own works to reduce its guilt or avoid its punishment. Nothing but repentance toward God and faith in Christ can save the sinner. The grace of Christ cannot be purchased—it is a free gift. He counseled the people not to buy indulgences but to look in faith to a crucified Redeemer. He told about his own painful experience and assured his hearers that it was by believing in Christ that he found peace and joy.

Does Forgiveness Free Us From Obedience?

Are we now free to disobey God's law? Paul says: "Do we then make void the law through faith? Certainly not! On the contrary,

---

* J. H. Merle D'Aubigne, *History of the Reformation of the Sixteenth Century,* book 2, chapter 3.
† *Ibid.,* book 2, chapter 4.

we establish the law" (Romans 3:31). "How shall we who died to sin live any longer in it?" (Romans 6:2). John declares: "This is the love of God, that we keep His commandments. And His commandments are not burdensome" (1 John 5:3). In the new birth the heart comes into harmony with God and His law. When this change has taken place, the sinner has passed from death into life, from law-breaking and rebellion to obedience and loyalty. The old life has ended; the new life of forgiveness, faith, and love has begun. Then "the righteous requirement of the law" will "be fulfilled in us who do not walk according to the flesh but according to the Spirit" (Romans 8:4). The language of the heart will be: "Oh, how I love Your law! It is my meditation all the day" (Psalm 119:97).

Without the law, people have no true conviction of sin and feel no need to repent. They do not realize how much they need the atoning blood of Christ. They accept the hope of salvation without a radical change of heart or reformation of life. So there are many superficial conversions, and many people who have never been united to Christ join the church.

What Is Sanctification?

Wrong ideas of sanctification also spring from neglecting or rejecting the divine law. These theories, involving false teachings and dangerous practical results, are often popular.

Paul wrote, "This is the will of God, your sanctification" (1 Thessalonians 4:3). The Bible clearly teaches what sanctification is and how we can attain it. The Savior prayed for His disciples: "Sanctify them by Your truth. Your word is truth" (John 17:17). And Paul taught that believers are to be "sanctified by the Holy Spirit" (Romans 15:16).

What is the work of the Holy Spirit? Jesus told His disciples, "When He, the Spirit of truth, has come, He will guide you into all truth" (John 16:13). And the psalmist says, "Your law is truth." Since the law of God is "holy and just and good," a character formed by obeying that law will be holy. Christ is a perfect example of a character like this. He says: "I have kept My Father's commandments"

(John 15:10). "I always do those things that please Him" (John 8:29). The followers of Christ are to become like Him—by the grace of God to form characters in harmony with the principles of His holy law. This is biblical sanctification.

Only Through Faith

We can accomplish this work only through faith in Christ, by the power of the Spirit of God living within us. Christians will feel sin tempting them, but they will keep up a constant warfare against it. They need Christ's help to do this. Human weakness unites with divine strength, and faith exclaims, "Thanks be to God, who gives us the victory through our Lord Jesus Christ" (1 Corinthians 15:57).

The work of sanctification is progressive. When the sinner finds peace with God at conversion, the Christian life has just begun. Now he is to "go on to perfection," to grow up "to the measure of the stature of the fullness of Christ" (Hebrews 6:1; Ephesians 4:13). "I press toward the goal for the prize of the upward call of God in Christ Jesus" (Philippians 3:14).

Those who experience the sanctification of the Bible will be humble. They see how unworthy they are in contrast with the purity and perfection of God. The prophet Daniel was an example of true sanctification. Instead of claiming to be pure and holy, this honored prophet identified himself with the really sinful of Israel as he pleaded before God for his people. (See Daniel 10:11; 9:15, 18, 20.)

Those who walk in the shadow of Calvary's cross will not exalt themselves or make boastful claims that they are free from sin. They feel that it was their sin that caused the agony that broke the heart of the Son of God, and this thought leads them to deep humility. Those who live closest to Jesus understand most clearly how frail and sinful humanity is, and their only hope is in the merit of a crucified and risen Savior.

The sanctification now gaining notice in the religious world carries a spirit of self-exaltation and a disregard for the law of God that identify it as foreign to the Bible. Those who teach it claim that sanctification happens instantly, and by this means, through "faith alone," they reach perfect holiness. "Only believe," they say, "and the blessing is yours." No further effort is supposed to be required from the receiver. At the same time they deny the authority of God's law, claiming that they are released from any obligation to keep the commandments. But is it possible to be holy without coming into harmony with the principles that express God's nature and will?

The Word of God testifies against this traplike doctrine of faith without works. It is not faith that claims God's favor without complying with the conditions on which He grants mercy. It is presumption. (See James 2:14-24.)

Let none deceive themselves that they can become holy while they willfully violate one of God's requirements. Known sin silences the witnessing voice of the Spirit and separates the heart from God. Though John dwells so much on love, he does not hesitate to reveal the true character of those who claim to be sanctified while living in violation of God's law. "He who says, 'I know Him,' and does not keep His commandments, is a liar, and the truth is not in him. But whoever keeps His word, truly the love of God is perfected in him" (1 John 2:4, 5). Here is the test of everyone's profession. If people belittle and make light of God's law, if they break "one of the least of these commandments" and teach others to do the same (Matthew 5:19), we may know that their claims have no foundation.

The claim to be without sin is evidence that the person who makes this claim is far from holy. Such a one has no true concept of God's infinite purity and holiness, and of how hateful and evil sin is. The greater the distance between us and Christ, the more righteous we appear in our own eyes.

Biblical Sanctification

Sanctification includes the entire being—spirit, soul, and body (see 1 Thessalonians 5:23). Christians are called to present their bodies "a living sacrifice, holy, acceptable to God" (Romans 12:1). Every practice that weakens physical or mental strength unfits us for the service of our Creator. Those who love God with all their heart will constantly try to bring every power of their being into harmony with the laws that make them better able to do His will. They will not weaken or defile the offering they present to their heavenly Father by indulging their appetites or passions.

Every sinful practice tends to numb and deaden the mental and spiritual understanding; the Word or Spirit of God can make only a feeble impression on the heart. "Let us cleanse ourselves from all filthiness of the flesh and spirit, perfecting holiness in the fear of God" (2 Corinthians 7:1).

How many professed Christians are degrading their godlike manhood or womanhood by gluttony, by wine drinking, by forbidden pleasure! And the church too often encourages the evil, to fill her treasury when love for Christ is too feeble to do it. If Jesus were to enter the churches of today and see the feasting that goes on there in the name of religion, would He not drive out those who desecrate His house that way, as He banished the moneychangers from the temple?

"Do you not know that your body is the temple of the Holy Spirit who is in you, whom you have from God, and you are not your own? For you were bought at a price; therefore glorify God in your body and in your spirit, which are God's" (1 Corinthians 6:19, 20). Christians whose bodies are the temple of the Holy Spirit will not be enslaved by an evil habit. Their powers belong to Christ. Their property is the Lord's. How could they squander this treasure that He has entrusted to them?

Every year professed Christians spend an immense amount of money on harmful pleasures. They rob God in tithes and offerings, while they consume on the altar of destroying lust more than they give to relieve the poor or support the gospel. If all who claim Christ's name were truly sanctified, they would give their money generously into the Lord's treasury instead of spending it for needless and hurtful indulgences. Christians would set an example of temperance and self-sacrifice. Then they would be the light of the world.

"The lust of the flesh, the lust of the eyes, and the pride of life" (1 John 2:16) control most people. But Christ's followers have a holier calling. "Come out from among them and be separate, says the Lord. Do not touch what is unclean." To those who comply with the conditions, God promises, "I will receive you. I will be a Father to you, and you shall be My sons and daughters, says the Lord Almighty" (2 Corinthians 6:17, 18).

Direct Access to God

Every step of faith and obedience brings the believer into closer connection with the Light of the World. The bright beams of the Sun of Righteousness shine on the servants of God, and they are to reflect His rays. The stars tell us that there is a light in heaven whose glory makes them bright. In the same way, Christians reveal to the world that there is a God on the throne whose character is worthy of praise and imitation. The holiness of His character will be visible in His witnesses.

Through the merits of Christ we have access to the throne of Infinite Power. "He who did not spare His own Son, but delivered Him up for us all, how shall He not with Him also freely give us all things?" (Romans 8:32). Jesus says: "If you then, being evil, know how to give good gifts to your children, how much more will your heavenly Father give the Holy Spirit to those who ask Him!" (Luke 11:13). "If you ask anything in My name, I will do it" (John 14:14). "Ask, and you will receive, that your joy may be full" (John 16:24).

It is the privilege of all to live in such a way that God will approve and bless them. It is not the will of our heavenly Father for us always to live in condemnation and darkness. It is not true humility if we go around with our heads bowed down and our hearts filled with thoughts of self. We may go to Jesus and be cleansed and stand before the law without shame and remorse.

Through Jesus the fallen sons of Adam become "sons of God." "He is not ashamed to call them brethren" (Hebrews 2:11). The Christian's life should be one of faith, victory, and joy in God. "The joy of the Lord is your strength" (Nehemiah 8:10). "Rejoice always, pray without ceasing, in everything give thanks; for this is the will of God in Christ Jesus for you" (1 Thessalonians 5:16-18).

These things are the fruits of Bible conversion and sanctification. It is only because people treat the great principles of righteousness shown in the law with such indifference that these fruits are so rare. This is why we see so little of that deep, lasting work of the Spirit that used to accompany revivals.

It is by beholding that we become changed. As people have neglected those sacred commandments in which God has revealed the perfection and holiness of His character, and their minds have been attracted to human teachings and theories, a decline of holy living in the church has followed. Only when the law of God is restored to its rightful position can a revival of authentic faith and godliness take place among His professed people.

Chapter 7

Our Only Safeguard

God points His followers to the Bible as their safeguard against the deceptive power of evil spirits. Satan uses every possible way to prevent people from gaining a knowledge of the Bible. At every revival of God's work, his activity becomes more intense. We will soon see a final struggle against Christ and His followers begin. The counterfeit will resemble the true so closely that it will be impossible to tell the difference between them except by the Scriptures.

Those who try to obey all of God's commandments will be opposed and mocked. To endure the trial, they must understand the will of God as revealed in His Word. They can honor Him only as they correctly understand His character, government, and goals, and act in harmony with them. Only those who have fortified their minds with the truths of the Bible will stand firmly through the last great struggle.

Before His crucifixion the Savior explained to His disciples that He was going to be killed and would rise again. Angels were there to impress His words on their minds and hearts. But they forgot the very words they needed to remember. When the trouble came, the death of Jesus destroyed their hopes as completely as if He had not warned them before. Similarly, the prophecies open the future before us as clearly as Christ opened it to the disciples. But most people have no more understanding of these important truths than if God had never revealed them.

When God sends warnings, He requires every sound-minded person to obey the message. The fearful judgments against worshiping the beast and his image (Revelation 14:9-11) should lead everyone to learn what the mark of the beast is and how to avoid receiving it.* But the great majority of people do not want Bible truth, because it goes against the desires of the sinful heart. Satan supplies them with the deceptions they love.

But God will have a people who hold the Bible, and the Bible only, as the standard of all doctrines and the basis of all reforms. The opinions of educated men, the conclusions of science, the decisions of church councils, the voice of the majority—not one nor all of these should we take as evidence for or against any doctrine. We should demand a plain "Thus says the Lord." Satan leads the people to look to pastors, to professors of theology, as their guides instead of searching the Scriptures for themselves. By controlling these leaders, he can influence most people.

When Christ came, the common people heard Him gladly. But the chief priests and the nation's leaders wrapped themselves in prejudice, rejecting the evidence that He was the Messiah. "How is it," the people asked, "that our rulers and enlightened scribes do not believe on Jesus?" Teachers like this led the Jewish nation to reject their Redeemer.

Exalting Human Authority

Christ foresaw that people would exalt human authority to rule over the conscience. In all ages this has been a terrible curse. As an appeal to future generations, the Bible recorded His warnings not to follow blind leaders.

The Roman Church teaches that only her clergy have the right to interpret the Scriptures. Though the Reformation gave the Scriptures to everyone, yet the same principle that Rome held prevents multitudes in Protestant churches from searching the Bible for themselves. They are taught to accept its teachings *as interpreted by the church.* Thousands do not dare to accept anything, no matter how plain it is in Scripture, that is contrary to their creed.

---

* This subject is presented in *The Great Controversy,* chapter 38.

Many are ready to commit their eternal destiny to the clergy. They pay almost no attention to the Savior's teachings. But are ministers infallible? How can we trust them to guide us unless we know from God's Word that they are light bearers? A lack of moral courage leads many to follow educated people, and they become hopelessly attached to error. They see the truth for this time in the Bible and feel the power of the Holy Spirit accompany the giving of it, yet they allow the clergy to turn them from the light.

Satan keeps many of his followers by attaching them with silken cords of affection to those who are enemies of the cross of Christ. This attachment may be to parents, brothers or sisters, husband or wife, or friends. Under their influence, many people do not have the courage to obey their convictions of what is right.

Many claim that it makes no difference what one believes, if that person lives the right life. But the life is molded by the faith. If truth is within reach and we neglect it, we are really rejecting it, choosing darkness rather than light.

Ignorance is no excuse for error or sin when we have every opportunity to know the will of God. A man who is traveling comes to a place where there are several roads and a signpost telling where each one leads. If he ignores the sign and takes whatever road seems to be right, he may be sincere, but he is likely to find himself on the wrong road.

The First and Highest Duty

It is not enough to have good intentions, to do what we think is right or what the minister tells us is right. We should search the Scriptures for ourselves. We have a map pointing out every key point on the journey to heaven, and we should not guess at anything.

It is the first and highest duty of every rational person to learn from the Scriptures what is truth, and then to walk in the light and encourage others to do the same. In our study, with God's help we are to form our opinions for ourselves, since we are to answer for ourselves before God.

Educated people, with a show of great wisdom, teach that the Scriptures have a secret, spiritual meaning that is not easily seen in the language used. They are false teachers. We should explain the language of the Bible by its obvious meaning, unless it uses a symbol or figure. If people would only take the Bible as it reads, it would accomplish a work that would bring thousands into the fold of Christ who now are wandering in error.

Many a Scripture which scholars ignore as unimportant is full of comfort to those who have been learning in the school of Christ. To understand Bible truth, we do not so much need the power of intellect for the search. Rather, we need a thirst for Bible truth more than anything else and an earnest longing for righteousness.

Results of Neglecting Prayer and Bible Study

We should never study the Bible without prayer. Only the Holy Spirit can cause us to feel the importance of things we understand easily or prevent us from twisting difficult truths. Heavenly angels prepare the heart to comprehend God's Word. We will be charmed with its beauty and strengthened by its promises. Temptations often seem irresistible because the tempted one cannot quickly remember God's promises and oppose Satan with the Scripture weapons. But angels are close to those willing to be taught, and they will bring to their memory the truths they need.

"He will teach you all things, and bring to your remembrance all things that I said to you" (John 14:26). But we must first store the teachings of Christ in the mind in order for the Spirit of God to bring them to our remembrance in the time of danger.

The destiny of all people on earth is about to be decided. Every follower of Christ should ask earnestly, "Lord, what do You want me to do?" (Acts 9:6). We should now seek a deep and living experience in the things of God. We have no time to lose. We are on Satan's territory. Sentinels of God, don't be caught sleeping!

Many congratulate themselves for the wrong acts that they do not commit. But it is not enough for them to be trees in the garden of

God. They are to bear fruit. In the books of heaven they are registered as those who use up the ground. Yet God's heart of long-suffering love still pleads with those who have despised His mercy and abused His grace.

In the summer there is no noticeable difference between evergreens and other trees. But when the storms of winter come, the evergreens remain unchanged while other trees lose their leaves. If opposition arises, intolerance again prevails, and persecution is kindled, the halfhearted and hypocritical will give up the faith. But the true Christians will stand firm, their faith stronger, their hope brighter, than in times of prosperity.

"He shall be like a tree planted by the waters, which spreads out its roots by the river, and will not fear when heat comes; but its leaf will be green, and will not be anxious in the year of drought, nor will cease from yielding fruit" (Jeremiah 17:8).

Chapter 8

In Defense of the Truth

The duty to worship God is based on the fact that He is the Creator. "Oh come, let us worship and bow down; let us kneel before the Lord our Maker" (Psalm 95:6; see Psalm 96:5; 100:3; Isaiah 40:25, 26; 45:18).

Revelation 14 calls people to worship the Creator and keep the commandments of God. One of these commandments points to God as the Creator: "The seventh day is the Sabbath of the Lord your God. . . . For in six days the Lord made the heavens and the earth, the sea, and all that is in them, and rested the seventh day. Therefore the Lord blessed the Sabbath day and hallowed it" (Exodus 20:10, 11). The Sabbath, the Lord says, is a "sign . . . , that you may know that I am the Lord your God" (Ezekiel 20:20). If everyone had kept the Sabbath, it would have led them to the Creator as the object of their worship. There would never have been an idol worshiper, atheist, or unbeliever. Keeping the Sabbath is a sign of loyalty to "Him who made heaven and earth, the sea and springs of water" (Revelation 14:7). The message that commands people to worship God and keep His commandments will especially call them to keep the fourth commandment.

Restoration of the Truth

Isaiah predicted Sabbath reform in the last days: "Thus says the Lord, 'Keep justice, and do righteousness, for My salvation is about to come, and My righteousness to be revealed. Blessed is the man who does this, and the son of man who lays hold on it; who keeps from defiling the Sabbath, and keeps his hand from doing any evil" (Isaiah

56:1, 2). "Also the sons of the foreigner who join themselves to the Lord, to serve Him, and to love the name of the Lord, to be His servants—everyone who keeps from defiling the Sabbath, and holds fast My covenant—even them I will bring to My holy mountain, and make them joyful in My house of prayer" (verses 6, 7).

These words apply in the Christian age, as the context shows: "The Lord God, who gathers the outcasts of Israel, says, 'Yet I will gather to him others besides those who are gathered to him'" (verse 8). This passage foreshadows the gospel's gathering in of the Gentiles, when His servants preach the good news to all nations.

The Lord commands, "Seal the law among my disciples" (Isaiah 8:16). The fourth commandment contains the seal of God's law. Only this commandment, of all the ten, includes both the name and the title of the Lawgiver. When the papal power tried to change the Sabbath,* this seal was removed from the law. God calls for the disciples of Jesus to restore it by exalting the Sabbath as the Creator's memorial and sign of His authority.

Protestants now claim that Christ's resurrection on Sunday made it the Christian Sabbath. But neither Christ nor His apostles gave any such honor to the day. Sunday observance had its origin in that "mystery of lawlessness" (2 Thessalonians 2:7) that had begun its work even in Paul's day. What reason can anyone give for a change that the Scriptures do not authorize?

Protestants admit that the New Testament is completely silent about "any explicit command for the Sabbath [referring here to Sunday, the first day of the week] or definite rules for its observance."†

"Up to the time of Christ's death, no change had been made in the day"; and "so far as the record shows, they [the apostles] did not . . . give any explicit command [to abandon] the seventh-day Sabbath, and [observe it] on the first day of the week."‡

---

* This change is described in chapter 3 of *The Great Controversy.*
† George Elliott, *The Abiding Sabbath,* p. 184.
‡ A. E. Waffle, *The Lord's Day,* pp. 186-188.

Roman Catholics acknowledge that their church made the change of the Sabbath, and they declare that Protestants recognize her power by observing Sunday. They claim, "During the old law, Saturday was the day sanctified; but *the church,* instructed by Jesus Christ, and directed by the Spirit of God, has substituted Sunday for Saturday; so now we sanctify the first, not the seventh day. Sunday means, and now is, the day of the Lord."*

God commands, "Cry aloud, spare not; lift up your voice like a trumpet; tell My people their transgression" (Isaiah 58:1). Those whom the Lord calls "My people" need to be told that they are breaking His law, even though they think that they are doing what is right in the service of God. But the solemn rebuke of the One who searches hearts shows that they are trampling on the divine commandments.

Here is how the prophet points out the law they have forsaken: "You shall raise up the foundations of many generations; and you shall be called the Repairer of the Breach, the Restorer of Streets to Dwell In. If you turn away your foot from the Sabbath, from doing your pleasure on My holy day; and call the Sabbath a delight, the holy day of the Lord honorable; and shall honor Him, not doing your own ways, nor finding your own pleasure, nor speaking your own words, then you shall delight yourself in the Lord" (verses 12-14). The "breach" in the law of God was made when the Roman power changed the Sabbath. But the time has come to repair the breach.

Adam kept the Sabbath in his innocence in Eden; he still kept it when, fallen yet repentant, he was driven from the Garden. All the patriarchs from Abel to Noah, to Abraham, to Jacob kept the Sabbath. When the Lord delivered Israel from Egypt, He proclaimed His law to the emerging nation.

True Sabbath Always Kept

From that day to now the Sabbath has been kept. Though the

---

* *Catholic Catechism of Christian Religion.*

"man of sin" succeeded in trampling God's holy day underfoot, yet faithful believers hidden in secret places paid it honor. Since the Reformation, some in every generation have kept it.

These truths found in Revelation 14 in connection with "the everlasting gospel" will distinguish the church of Christ at the time of His appearing. "Here are those who keep the commandments of God and the faith of Jesus" (Revelation 14:12).

Those who received the light about the sanctuary* and the law of God were filled with joy as they saw the harmony of truth. They wanted all Christians to have the light. But many who claimed to follow Christ did not welcome truths that were out of step with the world.

When they heard the claims of the Sabbath, many said: "We have always kept Sunday, our fathers kept it, and many good Christians have died happy while keeping it. The keeping of a new Sabbath would throw us out of harmony with the world. What can a little group keeping the seventh day accomplish against all the world who are keeping Sunday?" By arguments like these the Jews justified rejecting Christ. Similarly, in the time of Luther, Romanists reasoned that true Christians had died in the Catholic faith, so that religion was sufficient. Reasoning like this would stand in the way of every move forward in faith.

Many argued that Sundaykeeping had been a widespread custom of the church for centuries. Against this argument others showed that the Sabbath and its observance were older still, even as old as the world itself—established by the Ancient of Days.

When they could find no Bible support, many urged: "Why don't our great men understand this Sabbath question? Few believe as you do. It cannot be that you are right and all the educated people are wrong."

To refute arguments like these, it was enough just to quote the Scriptures and show how the Lord had dealt with His people in all

---

* See chapters 23 and 24 of *The Great Controversy.*

ages. The reason He does not more often choose people of learning and position to lead out in reform is that they trust to their creeds and theological systems and feel no need for God to teach them. God sometimes calls people to preach the truth who have little formal education. He chooses them, not because they are uneducated, but because they are not too self-sufficient for God to teach them. Their humility and obedience make them great.

Faith and Courage

It was not God's will for Israel to wander forty years in the wilderness. He wanted to lead them directly to Canaan and establish them there as a holy, happy people. But "they could not enter in because of unbelief" (Hebrews 3:19). In the same way, it was not God's will to delay the coming of Christ so long and to have His people remain so many years in this world of sin and sorrow. Unbelief separated them from God. In mercy to the world, Jesus delays His coming so that sinners may hear the warning and find shelter before God pours out His wrath.

Now as in earlier ages, presenting the truth will stir up opposition. With evil intent, many attack the character and motives of those who defend unpopular truth. Elijah was called a troubler in Israel, Jeremiah a traitor, Paul a polluter of the temple. From then until now, those who want to be loyal to truth have been denounced as rebellious, heretical, or divisive.

The confession of faith made by true believers and martyrs, those examples of holiness and firm integrity, inspires courage in those who are now called to stand as witnesses for God. The command comes to the servant of God today, "Lift up your voice like a trumpet; tell My people their transgression, and the house of Jacob their sins" (Isaiah 58:1). "I have made you a watchman for the house of Israel; therefore you shall hear a word from My mouth and warn them for Me" (Ezekiel 33:7).

The great obstacle to accepting truth is that it involves inconvenience and criticism. This is the only argument against the truth that those who defend truth have never been able to refute. But true followers of Christ do not wait for truth to become popular. They accept the cross, agreeing with Paul that "our light affliction, which is but for a moment, is working for us a far more exceeding and eternal weight of glory" (2 Corinthians 4:17); and with Moses, "esteeming the reproach of Christ greater riches than the treasures in Egypt" (Hebrews 11:26).

We should choose the right because it is right, and leave consequences with God. The world is indebted to people of principle, faith, and daring for its great reforms. The work of reform for this time must be carried forward by people like that.

Chapter 9

REAL HOPE

The promise of Christ's second coming to complete the great work of redemption is the main theme of the Sacred Scriptures. Since Adam and Eve left the Garden of Eden, the children of faith have waited for the coming of the Promised One to bring them to the lost Paradise again.

Enoch, the seventh generation from those who lived in Eden, who walked with God for three centuries, declared, "Behold, the Lord comes with ten thousands of His saints, to execute judgment on all" (Jude 14, 15). In the night of his suffering Job exclaimed, "I know that my Redeemer lives, and He shall stand at last on the earth; . . . in my flesh I shall see God, whom I shall see for myself, and my eyes shall behold, and not another" (Job 19:25-27). The poets and prophets of the Bible have written about the coming of Christ in words glowing with fire. "Let the heavens rejoice, and let the earth be glad" "before the Lord. For He is coming, for He is coming to judge the earth. He shall judge the world with righteousness, and the peoples with His truth" (Psalm 96:11-13).

Isaiah said: "It will be said in that day: 'Behold, this is our God; we have waited for Him, and He will save us. This is the Lord; we have waited for Him; we will be glad and rejoice in His salvation'" (Isaiah 25:9).

The Savior comforted His disciples with the assurance that He would come again: "In My Father's house are many mansions. . . . I go to prepare a place for you. And if I go . . . , I will come again and receive you to Myself" (John 14:2, 3). "When the Son of Man comes in His glory, and all the holy angels with Him, then He will sit on the throne of His glory. All the nations will be gathered before Him" (Matthew 25:31, 32).

Angels repeated to the disciples the promise of His return: "This *same* Jesus, who was taken up from you into heaven, will *so* come in like manner as you saw Him go into heaven" (Acts 1:11). And Paul testified: "The Lord *Himself* will descend from heaven with a shout, with the voice of an archangel, and with the trumpet of God" (1 Thessalonians 4:16). John, the prophet of Patmos, said: "Behold, He is coming with clouds, and every eye will see Him" (Revelation 1:7).

Then the agelong rule of evil will be broken: "The kingdoms of this world" will become "the kingdoms of our Lord and of His Christ, and He shall reign forever and ever!" (Revelation 11:15). "The Lord God will cause righteousness and praise to spring forth before all the nations" (Isaiah 61:11).

Then the peaceful kingdom of the Messiah will be established: "The Lord will comfort Zion, He will comfort all her waste places; He will make her wilderness like Eden, and her desert like the garden of the Lord" (Isaiah 51:3).

In all ages the coming of the Lord has been the hope of His true followers. In their suffering and persecution, the "appearing of our great God and Savior Jesus Christ" was the "blessed hope" (Titus 2:13). Paul pointed to the resurrection that will happen at the Savior's advent, when the dead in Christ will rise and be caught up together with the living to meet the Lord in the air. "And thus," he said, "we shall always be with the Lord. Therefore comfort one another with these words" (1 Thessalonians 4:17, 18).

On Patmos John, the beloved disciple, heard the promise "Surely I am coming quickly," and his response is the prayer of the church, "Even so, come, Lord Jesus!" (Revelation 22:20).

From the dungeon, the stake, the scaffold, where faithful believers and martyrs witnessed for the truth, comes down through the centuries the expression of their faith and hope. Being "assured of His personal resurrection, and consequently of their own resurrection at His coming, for this cause," says one of these Christians, "they despised death, and were found to be above it."* The Waldenses cherished the same faith. Wycliffe, Luther, Calvin, Knox, Ridley, and Baxter† looked in faith for the Lord's coming. This was the hope of the church in the apostles' time, of the "church in the wilderness," and of the Reformers.

Prophecy not only foretells the manner and purpose of Christ's second coming, but tells us how we may know when that day is near. "There will be signs in the sun, in the moon, and in the stars" (Luke 21:25). "The sun will be darkened, and the moon will not give its light; the stars of heaven will fall, and the powers in the heavens will be shaken. Then they will see the Son of Man coming in the clouds with great power and glory" (Mark 13:24-26). This is how John the revelator describes the first of the signs that come before the second advent: "There was a great earthquake; and the sun became black as sackcloth of hair, and the moon became like blood" (Revelation 6:12).

The Savior predicted the low spiritual condition of believers that would exist just before His second advent. Christ's counsel to those living at this time is: "Take heed to yourselves, lest your hearts be weighed down with carousing, drunkenness, and cares of this life, and that Day come on you unexpectedly" (Luke 21:34). "Watch therefore, and pray always that you may be counted worthy to escape all these things that will come to pass, and to stand before the Son of Man" (verse 36).

The Call to Prepare

With that great day approaching, the Word of God calls His people to turn to Him with repentance:

"The day of the Lord is coming, for it is at hand" (Joel 2:1). "Con-

---

* See Daniel T. Taylor, *The Reign of Christ on Earth: or, The Voice of the Church in All Ages,* p. 33.

† In the complete book, *The Great Controversy,* readers will find the story of the Waldenses and of these and other Protestant Reformers.

secrate a fast, call a sacred assembly; gather the people, sanctify the congregation, assemble the elders, gather the children. . . . Let the priests, who minister to the Lord, weep between the porch and the altar" (verses 15-17). " 'Turn to Me with all your heart, with fasting, with weeping, and with mourning.' So rend your heart, and not your garments; return to the Lord your God, for He is gracious and merciful, slow to anger, and of great kindness" (verses 12, 13).

To prepare a people to stand in the day of God, there was a great work of reform to be done. In His mercy God was about to send a message to awaken those who claimed to be His people and lead them to get ready for the coming of the Lord.

We find this warning in Revelation 14. Here is a three-part message represented as proclaimed by heavenly beings and followed immediately by the Son of man's coming to reap "the harvest of the earth" (Revelation 14:15). The prophet saw an angel "flying in the midst of heaven, having the everlasting gospel to preach to those who dwell on the earth—to every nation, tribe, tongue, and people—saying with a loud voice, 'Fear God and give glory to Him, for the hour of His judgment has come; and worship Him who made heaven and earth, the sea and springs of water' " (verses 6, 7).

This message is a part of "the everlasting gospel." God has entrusted the work of preaching to us. Holy angels direct, but the servants of Christ on earth actually proclaim the gospel.*

Danger of Resisting the Gospel Call

The destruction of Jerusalem is a solemn warning to everyone who is resisting the pleadings of God's mercy. The Savior's prophecy of judgments on Jerusalem is to have another fulfillment. In the fate of that chosen city we can see the doom of a world that has rejected God's mercy and trampled on His law. Dark are the records of

---

* For a more detailed account of this message and of those who began to proclaim it, see *The Great Controversy,* chapters 17 and 18, and subsequent chapters that develop the issues further.

human misery that the earth has witnessed. Terrible have been the results of rejecting Heaven's authority. But a scene still darker is presented in the revelations of the future. When the restraining Spirit of God will be completely withdrawn, no longer holding back the outburst of human passion and satanic anger, the world will see the results of Satan's rule as it has never seen them before.

In that day, as when Jerusalem was destroyed, God's people will be delivered. Christ will come the second time to gather His faithful ones to Himself. "Then all the tribes of the earth will mourn, and they will see the Son of Man coming on the clouds of heaven with power and great glory. And He will send His angels with a great sound of a trumpet, and they will gather together His elect from the four winds, from one end of heaven to the other" (Matthew 24:30, 31).

People should be careful not to neglect the words of Christ. As He warned His disciples of Jerusalem's destruction so that they could escape, so He has warned the world of the day of final destruction. All who choose may flee from the wrath to come. "There will be signs in the sun, in the moon, and in the stars; and on the earth distress of nations" (Luke 21:25; see also Matthew 24:29; Mark 13:24-26; Revelation 6:12-17). "Watch therefore" are Christ's words of counsel (Mark 13:35). Those who obey the warning will not be left in darkness.

The world is no more ready to believe the message for this time than the Jews were to receive the Savior's warning about Jerusalem. No matter when it comes, the day of God will come as a surprise to the ungodly. When life is going on in its usual way, when people are absorbed in pleasure, in business, in moneymaking, when religious leaders are praising the world's progress, and people are lulled in a false security—then, as the midnight thief slips into the unguarded home, so shall sudden destruction come upon the careless and ungodly, "and they shall not escape" (1 Thessalonians 5:3).

Satan Tries to Keep People in His Power

Through the two great errors, the immortality of the soul and

Sunday sacredness, Satan will bring the people under his deceptions. While the immortality of the soul lays the foundation of spiritualism, Sunday sacredness creates ties of sympathy with Rome.

Through spiritualism Satan appears to be someone who blesses humanity, healing diseases and presenting a new system of religious faith, but at the same time he leads many people to ruin. Alcohol use overcomes reason; sensual indulgence, conflict, and bloodshed follow. War stirs up the worst passions of the heart and sweeps its victims into eternity, covered in vice and blood. It is Satan's goal to prod the nations to war, because in this way he can divert people from preparing for the judgment and eternity.

Satan has studied the secrets of nature, and he uses all his power to control the elements as far as God allows. It is God who shields His creatures from the destroyer. But the Christian world has shown contempt for His law, and the Lord will do what He said He would—remove His protecting care from those who rebel against His law and who force others to do the same. Satan has control of everyone whom God does not especially guard. He will favor and prosper some in order to advance his own plans, and he will bring trouble on others and lead them to believe that God is the one who is mistreating them.

While appearing to be a great physician who can heal all their illnesses, Satan will bring disease and disaster until crowded cities are reduced to ruin. In accidents by sea and land, in great fires, in fierce tornadoes and hailstorms, in gales, floods, hurricanes, tidal waves, and earthquakes, in a thousand forms, Satan is exerting his power. He sweeps away the ripening harvest, and famine and misery follow. He gives the air a deadly taint, and thousands die.

And then the great deceiver will persuade people to blame all their troubles on those whose obedience to God's commandments is a constant rebuke to those who break God's law. They will say that these people are offending God by violating Sunday, and that this sin has brought disasters that will not stop until Sunday observance is strictly enforced. They will claim that those who destroy reverence for Sunday are preventing their restoration to God's favor and material prosperity. They will repeat the accusation urged long ago against the servant of God: "When Ahab saw Elijah, Ahab said to him, 'Is it you, you troubler of Israel?'" (1 Kings 18:17, NRSV).

Those who honor the Bible Sabbath will be blamed as enemies of law and order, breaking down the moral restraints of society, causing lawlessness and corruption, and calling down the judgments of God on the earth. They will be accused of undermining the government. Ministers who deny that people need to keep God's law will preach about the duty of obeying the civil authorities. In legislative halls and courts of justice, commandment keepers will be condemned. People will put a false slant on their words and the worst construction on their motives.

Leaders of church and state will unite to persuade or force everyone to honor Sunday. Even in free America rulers and legislators will give in to the popular demand for a law enforcing Sunday observance. Liberty of conscience, which has cost so great a sacrifice, will no longer be respected. In the soon-coming conflict we will see the prophet's words fulfilled: "The dragon was enraged with the woman, and he went to make war with the rest of her offspring, who keep the commandments of God and have the testimony of Jesus Christ" (Revelation 12:17).

Servants of God, their faces shining with holy devotion, will hurry from place to place to tell the message from heaven. Miracles will take place, the sick will be healed. Satan also works with deceptive miracles, even bringing down fire from heaven (Revelation 13:13). These things will move the inhabitants of the earth to choose sides.

The message will succeed not so much by argument as by the deep conviction of the Spirit of God. The arguments have been presented, publications have exerted their influence, yet Satan has kept many from fully understanding the truth. Now they see the truth in its clearness. Family relationships and church connections are powerless to stop the honest children of God now. Regardless of the forces combined against the truth, a large number take their stand on the Lord's side.

People will think that those who honor the law of God are the cause of the fearful conflict and bloodshed that fill the earth with misery. The power that accompanies the last warning has enraged the wicked, and Satan will stir up the spirit of hatred and persecution against all who have received the message.

A Faith That Endures

The time of distress and anguish ahead of us will require a faith that can endure weariness, delay, and hunger, a faith that will not crumble even though it is tested severely. Jacob's victory (see Gen. 32:24-30) is an evidence of the power of persistent prayer. All who will lay hold of God's promises, as Jacob did, will succeed as he succeeded. Wrestling with God—how few know what it is! When waves of despair sweep over the needy, praying ones, how few cling with faith to the promises of God.

Fearful sights of a supernatural kind will soon appear in the heavens, in support of the power of miracle-working demons. Spirits of demons will go out to the "kings of the earth" and to the whole world, to urge them to unite with Satan in his last struggle against the government of heaven. People will come forward, pretending to be Christ Himself. They will perform miracles of healing and profess to have revelations from heaven that contradict the Scriptures.

The Crowning Act

As the crowning act in the great drama of deception, Satan himself will appear as if he were Christ. The church has long looked for the Savior's coming as the fulfillment of her hopes. Now the great deceiver will make it appear that Christ has come. Satan will show himself as a majestic being of dazzling brightness, resembling the description of the Son of God in the book of Revelation (Revelation 1:13-15).

The glory that surrounds him is greater than anything that mortal eyes have yet seen. The shout of triumph rings out, "Christ has come!" The people bow down before him. He lifts up his hands and blesses them. His voice is soft, yet full of melody. In compassionate tones he presents some of the same heavenly truths the Savior spoke. He heals diseases, and then, in his assumed character of Christ, claims to have changed the Sabbath to Sunday. He declares that those who keep holy the seventh day are showing contempt for him. This is the strong, almost overpowering delusion. Vast numbers believe his sorceries, saying, This is "the great power of God" (Acts 8:10).

God's People Not Misled

But the people of God will not be misled. The teachings of this false christ are not in harmony with the Scriptures. He pronounces his blessing on the worshipers of the beast and his image, the very class on whom the Bible says that God will pour out His undiluted wrath.

Furthermore, God does not permit Satan to counterfeit the manner of Christ's coming. The Savior warned His people against being deceived on this point. "False christs and false prophets will rise and show great signs and wonders to deceive, if possible, even the elect. . . . Therefore if they say to you, 'Look, He is in the desert!' do not go out; or 'Look, He is in the inner rooms!' do not believe it. For as the lightning comes from the east and flashes to the west, so also will the coming of the Son of Man be" (Matthew 24:24-27; see also Matthew 25:31; Revelation 1:7; 1 Thessalonians 4:16, 17). This coming is impossible to counterfeit. The whole world will witness it.

Only those who have studied the Scriptures diligently and have received the love of the truth will be shielded from the powerful deception that takes the world captive. By the Bible testimony, they will detect the deceiver in his disguise. Are the people of God now so firmly established on His Word that they would not give in to the evidence of their senses? In such a crisis, would they cling to the Bible, and the Bible only?

Chapter 10

THE GREAT RESCUE

When the protection of human laws is withdrawn from those who honor the law of God, in different lands there will be a simultaneous movement to destroy them. As the time set in the decree approaches, the people will conspire to strike in one night a decisive blow that will silence dissent and reproof.

The people of God—some in prison cells, some in forests and mountains—plead for divine protection. Armed men, urged on by evil angels, are preparing for the work of death. Now, in the hour of greatest extremity, God will step in: "You shall have a song as in the night when a holy festival is kept; and gladness of heart as when one goes . . . to come into the mountain of the Lord, to the Mighty One of Israel. The Lord will cause His glorious voice to be heard, and show the descent of His arm, with the indignation of His anger and the flame of a devouring fire, with scattering, tempest, and hailstones" (Isaiah 30:29, 30).

Mobs of evil men are about to rush upon their prey, when a dense blackness, deeper than night, falls on the earth. Then a rainbow spans the sky and seems to encircle each praying group. The angry crowds are stopped. They forget the objects of their rage. They gaze on the symbol of God's covenant, and they long to be shielded from its brightness.

The people of God hear a voice saying, "Look up." Like Stephen, the early Christian martyr, they look up and see the glory of God and the Son of man on His throne (see Acts 7:55, 56). They recognize the marks of His humiliation, and they hear His request, "I desire that they also whom You gave Me may be with Me where

I am" (John 17:24). They hear a voice saying, "They come, holy, harmless, and undefiled! They have kept My command to persevere."

Deliverance Comes

At midnight God unveils His power to deliver His people. The sun appears shining in its strength. Signs and wonders follow. The wicked look with terror on the scene, while the righteous see the indications of their deliverance. In the midst of the angry sky is one clear space of indescribable glory. The voice of God comes from there like the sound of many waters, saying, "It is done!" (Revelation 16:17).

That voice shakes the heavens and the earth. There is a mighty earthquake, "such a mighty and great earthquake as had not occurred since men were on the earth" (verse 18). Ragged rocks are scattered on every side. The sea is lashed into fury. There is the shriek of a hurricane like the voice of demons. The earth's surface is breaking up. Its very foundations seem to be giving way. Seaports that have become like Sodom for wickedness are swallowed up by the angry waters. "Babylon the great" is "remembered before God, to give her the cup of the wine of the fierceness of His wrath" (verse 19). Great hailstones do their work of destruction. Proud cities are laid low. Grand palaces on which people have lavished their wealth crumble before their eyes. Prison walls are torn apart, and God's people are set free.

Graves are opened, and "many of those who sleep in the dust of the earth . . . awake, some to everlasting life, some to shame and everlasting contempt" (Daniel 12:2). "Even they who pierced Him" (Revelation 1:7), those who mocked Christ's dying agonies, and the most violent opposers of His truth, are raised to see the honor placed on the loyal and obedient.

Fierce lightnings wrap the earth in a sheet of flame. Above the thunder, voices—mysterious and awful—declare the doom of the wicked. Those who were boastful and defiant, cruel to God's commandment-keeping people, now shudder in fear. Demons tremble while men and women beg for mercy.

The Day of the Lord

The prophet Isaiah said: "In that day a man will cast away his idols of silver and his idols of gold, which they made, each for himself to worship, to the moles and bats, to go into the clefts of the rocks, and into the crags of the rugged rocks, from the terror of the Lord and the glory of His majesty, when He arises to shake the earth mightily" (Isaiah 2:20, 21).

Those who have sacrificed everything for Christ are now safe. Before the world and in the face of death they have demonstrated their loyalty to Him who died for them. Their faces, so recently pale and gaunt, are now aglow with awe. Their voices rise in triumphant song: "God is our refuge and strength, a very present help in trouble. Therefore we will not fear, even though the earth be removed, and though the mountains be carried into the midst of the sea; though its waters roar and be troubled, though the mountains shake with its swelling" (Psalm 46:1-3).

While these words of holy trust ascend to God, the glory of the celestial city streams from heaven's open gates. Then, against the sky, a hand appears, holding two tablets of stone. That holy law, which God spoke from Sinai, is now revealed as the rule of judgment. The words are so plain that everyone can read them, and they awaken memories that sweep the darkness of superstition and heresy from every mind.

It is impossible to describe the horror and despair of those who have trampled on God's law. To gain the approval of the world, they set aside the law's requirements and taught others to disobey it. Now that law which they have despised condemns them. They see that they are without excuse. The enemies of God's law have a new understanding of truth and duty. Too late they see that the Sabbath is the seal of the living God. Too late they see the sandy foundation on which they have been building. They have been fighting against God. Religious teachers have led people to destruction while claiming to guide them to Paradise. How great is the responsibility of those in holy office, how terrible the results of their unfaithfulness!

The King of Kings Appears

The voice of God is heard declaring the day and hour of Jesus' coming. The people of God stand listening, their faces lighted up with His glory. Soon in the east a small black cloud appears. It is the cloud that surrounds the Savior. In solemn silence the people of God gaze at it as it comes nearer, until it is a great white cloud, its base a glory like consuming fire, and above it the rainbow of the covenant. Not now a "Man of sorrows," Jesus rides forward as a mighty conqueror. Holy angels, a vast crowd of them too many to count, come with Him, "ten thousand times ten thousand, and thousands of thousands" (Revelation 5:11). Every eye sees the Prince of life. A crown of glory rests on His brow. His face is brighter than the noonday sun. "And He has on His robe and on His thigh a name written: KING OF KINGS AND LORD OF LORDS" (Revelation 19:16).

The King of kings descends on the cloud, wrapped in flaming fire. The earth trembles before Him: "Our God shall come, and shall not keep silent; a fire shall devour before Him, and it shall be very tempestuous all around Him. He shall call to the heavens from above, and to the earth, that He may judge His people" (Psalm 50:3, 4).

"And the kings of the earth, the great men, the rich men, the commanders, the mighty men, every slave and every free man, hid themselves in the caves and in the rocks of the mountains, and said to the mountains and rocks, 'Fall on us and hide us from the face of Him who sits on the throne and from the wrath of the Lamb! For the great day of His wrath has come, and who is able to stand?'" (Revelation 6:15-17).

Mocking jokes have ended, lying lips hushed. Nothing is heard except the voice of prayer and the sound of weeping. The wicked pray to be buried beneath the rocks rather than have to face Him whom they have despised. That voice which penetrates the ear of the dead, they know. How often its tender tones have called them to repentance! How often they have heard it in the appeals of a friend, a brother, a Redeemer. Oh, if only it were the voice of a stranger to them! That voice awakens memories of warnings they despised and invitations they refused.

Those who mocked Christ in His humiliation are there. He declared, "Hereafter you will see the Son of Man sitting at the right hand of the Power, and coming on the clouds of heaven" (Matthew 26:64). Now they look at Him in His glory; they are yet to see Him sitting at the right hand of power. There is the haughty Herod who jeered at His royal title. There are the men who placed the thorny crown on His brow and the mimic scepter in His hand—those who bowed before Him in blasphemous mockery, who spat on the Prince of life. They try to run from His presence. Those who drove the nails through His hands and feet gaze at these marks with terror and remorse.

With terrible clarity priests and rulers remember the events of Calvary, how, wagging their heads in satanic gloating, they exclaimed, "He saved others; Himself He cannot save" (Matthew 27:42). Louder than the shout "Crucify Him, crucify Him!" which rang through Jerusalem, swells the despairing wail "He is the Son of God!" They try to run from the presence of the King of kings.

In the lives of all who reject truth there are moments when conscience wakes up, when the mind is troubled with vain regrets. But what are these compared with the remorse of that day! In the midst of their terror they hear the voices of the redeemed exclaiming, "Behold, this is our God; we have waited for Him, and He will save us" (Isaiah 25:9).

Resurrection of God's People

The voice of the Son of God calls the sleeping saints from their graves. Throughout the earth the dead will hear that voice, and they that hear will live, a great army of every nation, tribe, tongue, and people. From the prison house of death they come, clothed with immortal glory, crying out: "O Death, where is your sting? O Hades, where is your victory?" (1 Corinthians 15:55).

All come out from their graves the same height as when they entered the tomb. But all arise with the freshness and vigor of eternal youth. Christ came to restore what was lost. He will change our lowly bodies and conform them to His glorious body. The mortal, corruptible form, once polluted with sin, becomes perfect, beautiful and immortal. Blemishes and deformities are left in the grave. The redeemed will "grow up" (Malachi 4:2, KJV) to the full stature of the race in its original glory. The last lingering traces of the curse of sin will be removed. In mind and soul and body, Christ's faithful ones will reflect the perfect image of their Lord.

The living righteous are changed "in a moment, in the twinkling of an eye" (1 Corinthians 15:52). At the voice of God they are made immortal, and with the risen redeemed they are caught up to meet their Lord in the air. Angels "gather together His elect from the four winds, from one end of heaven to the other" (Matthew 24:31). They carry little children to their mothers' arms. Friends long separated by death are united, never to part again, and with songs of gladness they ascend together to the City of God.

Into the Holy City

Throughout the countless numbers of the redeemed every gaze is fastened on Jesus. Every eye beholds the glory of Him whose "visage was marred more than any man, and His form more than the sons of men" (Isaiah 52:14). Jesus places the crown of glory on the heads of the overcomers. For each there is a crown bearing his own "new name" (Revelation 2:17) and the inscription "Holiness to the Lord." Every hand receives the victor's palm and the shining harp. Then, as the commanding angels strike the note, all the redeemed sweep the strings with skillful touch in rich, melodious tones. Each voice is raised in grateful praise: "To him who loved us and washed us from our sins in His own blood, and has made us kings and

priests to His God and Father, to Him be glory and dominion forever and ever" (Revelation 1:5, 6).

Just ahead of the assembled redeemed is the Holy City. Jesus
opens the gates, and the people from all nations who have kept the
truth enter in. Then He says, "Come, you blessed of My Father, inherit the kingdom prepared for you from the foundation of the
world" (Matthew 25:34). Christ presents to the Father those His
blood has purchased, declaring: "Here am I and the children whom
God has given me" (Hebrews 2:13). "Those whom You gave Me I
have kept" (John 17:12). Oh, the joy of that moment when the infinite Father, looking at the ransomed, will see His image, sin's
decay removed, and the human once more in harmony with the divine!

The Savior's joy is in seeing, in the kingdom of glory, the people
who have been saved by His agony and humiliation. The redeemed
will share in His joy, as they see others who were won through their
prayers, labors, and loving sacrifice. Gladness will fill their hearts
when they see that one has brought others, and these still others.

The Two Adams Meet

As the ransomed are welcomed to the City of God, a triumphant
cry rings out. The two Adams are about to meet. The Son of God
will receive the father of our race—whom He created, who sinned,
and for whose sin the marks of the crucifixion are on the Savior's
body. As Adam sees the prints of the nails, in humiliation he throws
himself at Christ's feet. The Savior lifts him up and invites him to
look once more on the Eden home from which he was exiled so long
ago.

Adam's life was filled with sorrow. Every dying leaf, every animal
sacrifice, every stain on humanity's purity, was a reminder of his sin.
His agony of remorse was terrible, as he was blamed for being the
cause of sin. Faithfully he repented of his sin, and he died in the
hope of a resurrection. Now, through the atonement, Adam is reinstated in his Eden home.

Filled with joy, he sees the trees that were once his delight, whose fruit he himself had gathered in the days of his innocence. He sees the vines his own hands trained, the very flowers he once loved to care for. This is truly Eden restored!

The Savior leads him to the tree of life and invites him to eat. He sees so many of his family redeemed. Then he throws his crown at the feet of Jesus and embraces the Redeemer. He touches the harp, and heaven echoes the triumphant song, "Worthy is the Lamb who was slain" (Revelation 5:12). The family of Adam throw their crowns at the Savior's feet as they bow in adoration. Angels wept when Adam sinned, and they rejoiced when Jesus opened the grave for all who would believe on His name. Now they see the work of redemption accomplished, and they unite their voices in praise.

On the "sea of glass mingled with fire" are gathered those who have gotten "the victory over the beast, over his image and over his mark and over the number of his name" (Revelation 15:2). The one hundred forty-four thousand were redeemed from among humanity, and they sing "a new song," the song of Moses and the Lamb. None but the hundred forty-four thousand can learn that song, because it is the song of an experience that no other group ever had (Revelation 14:3; 15:3). "These are the ones who follow the Lamb wherever He goes." These, having been taken to heaven from among the living, are the "firstfruits to God and to the Lamb" (Revelation 14:4). They passed through the time of trouble such as never was since there was a nation. They endured the anguish of the time of Jacob's trouble. They stood without an intercessor through the final outpouring of God's judgments. They "washed their robes and made them white in the blood of the Lamb" (Revelation 7:14). "In their mouth was found no deceit, for they are without fault" before God (Revelation 14:5). "They shall neither hunger anymore nor thirst anymore; the sun shall not strike them, nor any heat; for the Lamb who is in the midst of the throne will shepherd them and lead them to living fountains of waters. And God will wipe away every tear from their eyes" (Revelation 7:16, 17).

The Redeemed in Glory

In all ages the Savior's chosen ones have walked in narrow paths. They were purified in the fires of affliction. For Jesus' sake they endured hatred, slander, self-denial, and bitter disappointments. They learned the evil of sin, its power, its guilt, its misery. They abhor it now. A sense of Jesus' infinite sacrifice for its cure humbles them and fills their hearts with gratitude. They love much because they have been forgiven much (see Luke 7:47). Partakers of Christ's sufferings, they are prepared to be partakers of His glory.

The heirs of God come from attics, hovels, dungeons, scaffolds, mountains, deserts, caves. They were "destitute, afflicted, tormented." Millions went to the grave dishonored by nearly everyone because they refused to yield to Satan. But now they are no longer afflicted, scattered, and oppressed. From this point onward they stand dressed in richer robes than the most honored of the earth have worn, wearing crowns more glorious than were ever placed on the head of earthly rulers. The King of glory has wiped the tears from all faces. They join in a song of praise, clear, sweet, and harmonious. The anthem swells throughout heaven, "Salvation belongs to our God who sits on the throne, and to the Lamb!" (Revelation 7:10). And all respond, "Amen! Blessing and glory and wisdom, thanksgiving and honor and power and might, be to our God forever and ever" (verse 12).

In this life we can only begin to understand the wonderful theme of redemption. With our limited comprehension we may consider very earnestly the shame and the glory, the life and the death, the justice and the mercy, that meet in the cross. Yet even with the greatest stretch of our mental powers, we fail to grasp its full significance. The length and the breadth, the depth and the height, of redeeming love we only dimly comprehend. The plan of redemption will not be fully understood even when the ransomed see as they are seen and know as they are known, but through the eternal ages new truth will continually unfold to their amazed and delighted minds. Though the griefs and pains and temptations of earth are over and their cause removed, the people of God will always have a distinct, intelligent knowledge of what their salvation has cost.

The cross will be the song of the redeemed through all eternity. In Christ glorified they see Christ crucified. They will never forget that the Majesty of heaven humbled Himself to uplift fallen men and women, that He bore the guilt and shame of sin and the hiding of His Father's face till the anguish of a lost world broke His heart and crushed out His life. The Maker of all worlds laid aside His glory from love to humanity—this will forever inspire the awe of the universe. As the nations of the saved look on their Redeemer and know that His kingdom will have no end, they break out in song: "Worthy is the Lamb that was slain, and has redeemed us to God by His own most precious blood!"

The mystery of the cross explains all mysteries. It will be clear that God who is infinite in wisdom could invent no plan for our salvation except by the sacrifice of His Son. His compensation for this sacrifice is the joy of peopling the earth with ransomed beings, holy, happy, and immortal. So great is the value of each person that the Father is satisfied with the price paid. And Christ Himself, seeing the fruits of His great sacrifice, is satisfied.

Chapter 11

VICTORY OF LOVE

At the close of the thousand years,* Christ returns to the earth accompanied by the redeemed and by legions of angels. He commands the wicked dead to arise to receive their doom. They come out, numberless as the sands of the sea, bearing the traces of disease and death. What a contrast to those raised in the first resurrection!

Every eye turns to see the glory of the Son of God. With one voice the vast army of the wicked exclaims, "Blessed is He who comes in the name of the Lord!" (Matthew 23:39). It is not love that inspires this utterance. The force of truth urges the words from unwilling lips. As the wicked went into the graves, so they come out with the same hatred of Christ and the same spirit of rebellion. They will have no new probation in which to remedy their past lives.

Says the prophet, "In that day His feet will stand on the Mount of Olives, . . . and the Mount of Olives shall be split in two" (Zechariah 14:4). As the New Jerusalem comes down out of heaven, it rests on the place made ready for it, and Christ, with His people and the angels, enters the Holy City.

While he was cut off from his work of deception, the prince of evil was miserable and dejected, but when the wicked dead are raised and he sees the vast forces on his side, his hopes revive. He determines not to give up the great controversy. He will rally the lost under his banner. In rejecting Christ they have accepted the rule of

---

* This is the millennium, described in the Bible in Revelation 20:1-6 and in the complete book, *The Great Controversy,* chapter 41.

the rebel leader, and they are ready to do his bidding. Yet, true to his early practice, he does not acknowledge himself to be Satan. He claims to be the rightful owner of the world whose inheritance has been taken from him unlawfully. He represents himself as a redeemer, assuring his deluded subjects that it is his power that has brought them from their graves. Satan makes the weak strong and inspires all with his own energy. He proposes to lead them in battle to take possession of the City of God. He points to the unnumbered millions who have been raised from the dead, and he declares that as their leader he is well able to regain his throne and kingdom.

In the vast assembly are many from the long-lived race that existed before the Flood, people of tall stature and giant intellect, whose amazing works led the world to idolize their genius, but whose cruelty and evil practices caused God to blot them from His creation. There are kings and generals who never lost a battle. In death these leaders experienced no change. As they come up from the grave, they are driven by the same desire to conquer that ruled them when they died.

The Final Assault Against God

Satan consults with these mighty men. They declare that the army within the city is small in comparison with theirs and can be overcome. Skillful craftsmen construct weapons of war. Military leaders marshal warlike men into companies and divisions.

At last the order to advance is given, and the countless horde moves on, an army that the combined forces of all ages could never equal. Satan leads the procession, kings and warriors following. With military precision the densely packed ranks advance over the earth's broken surface to the City of God. By command of Jesus, the gates of the New Jerusalem are closed, and the armies of Satan prepare for the attack.

Now Christ appears in view of His enemies. Far above the city, on a foundation of burnished gold, is a throne. The Son of God sits on this throne, and around Him are the subjects of His kingdom. The glory of the Eternal Father enfolds His Son. The brightness of His presence flows out beyond the gates, flooding the earth with radiance.

Nearest the throne are those who were once zealous in Satan's cause, but who, plucked like brands from the fire, have followed their Savior with intense devotion. Next are those who perfected character while surrounded by falsehood and unbelief, who honored the law of God when the world declared it void, and the millions from all ages who were martyred for their faith. Beyond is the "great multitude which no one could number, of all nations, tribes, peoples, and tongues, . . . clothed with white robes, with palm branches in their hands" (Revelation 7:9). Their warfare is over, their victory won. The palm branch is a symbol of triumph, the white robe an emblem of the righteousness of Christ, which is now theirs.

In all that vast crowd there are none who credit salvation to themselves by their own goodness. Nothing is said of what they have suffered. The keynote of every anthem is: Salvation to our God and to the Lamb.

Sentence Pronounced Against the Rebels

In the presence of the assembled inhabitants of earth and heaven the coronation of the Son of God takes place. And now, acknowledged as having supreme majesty and power, the King of kings pronounces sentence on the rebels who have broken His law and oppressed His people. "I saw a great white throne and Him who sat on it, from whose face the earth and the heaven fled away. And there was found no place for them. And I saw the dead, small and great, standing before God, and books were opened. And another book was opened, which is the Book of Life. And the dead were judged according to their works, by the things which were written in the books" (Revelation 20:11, 12).

As the eye of Jesus looks upon the wicked, they are conscious of every sin they have ever committed. They see where their feet left the path of holiness. The alluring temptations that they encouraged by indulging in sin, the messengers of God they despised, the warnings they rejected, the waves of mercy that their stubborn, unrepentant hearts beat back—all appear as if written in letters of fire.

Above the throne they see the cross. Like a panoramic view they watch the scenes of Adam's fall and the steps that followed it in the plan of redemption. The Savior's humble birth; His life of simplicity; His baptism in the Jordan; His fasting and temptation in the wilderness; His ministry bringing heaven's blessings to humanity; the days crowded with acts of mercy, the nights of prayer in the mountains; the plottings of envy and meanness that repaid His benefits; His mysterious agony in Gethsemane beneath the weight of the sins of the world; His betrayal to the murderous mob; the events of that night of horror—the unresisting prisoner abandoned by His disciples, put on trial in the high priest's palace, in the judgment hall of Pilate, before the cowardly Herod, mocked, insulted, tortured, and condemned to die—these events are all vividly portrayed.

And now the swaying crowd watches the final scenes: the patient Sufferer treading the path to Calvary; the Prince of heaven hanging on the cross; the priests and rabbis mocking His dying agony; the supernatural darkness marking the moment when the world's Redeemer yielded up His life.

The awful spectacle appears just as it was. Satan and his subjects have no power to turn away from the picture. Each actor remembers the part he performed. Herod, who killed the innocent children of Bethlehem; the evil Herodias, guilty of the blood of John the Baptist; the weak, political Pilate; the mocking soldiers; the raging crowd who shouted, "His blood be on us and on our children!"—all try but fail to hide from the divine majesty of His face, while the redeemed throw their crowns at the Savior's feet, exclaiming, "He died for me!"

There is Nero, monster of cruelty and vice, watching the exaltation of those Christians in whose dying anguish he found satanic delight. His mother witnesses her own work, how the passions that her influence and example encouraged have borne fruit in crimes that made the world shudder.

There are Catholic priests and officials who claimed to be Christ's ambassadors, yet used the rack, the dungeon, and the stake to control His people. There are the proud popes who exalted themselves above God and dared to try to change the law of the Most High. Those pretended fathers have an account to settle with God. Too late they are made to see that the All-knowing One is particular about His law. They learn now that Christ identifies His interests with His suffering people.

The whole wicked world stands arraigned on the charge of high treason against the government of heaven. The lost have no one to plead their cause. They are without excuse, and God pronounces the sentence of eternal death against them.

The wicked see what they have forfeited by their rebellion. "All this," cries the lost sinner, "I might have had. Why was I so blind! I have exchanged peace, happiness, and honor for wretchedness, disgrace, and despair." All see that God is just in excluding them from heaven. By their lives they have declared, "We will not have this man [Jesus] to reign over us" (see Luke 19:14).

Satan Defeated

As if hypnotized, the wicked watch the coronation of the Son of God. They see in His hands the tablets of the divine law they have despised. They witness the outburst of adoration from the saved; and as the wave of melody sweeps over the crowds outside the city, all exclaim, "Just and true are Your ways, O King of the saints!" (Revelation 15:3). Falling facedown, they worship the Prince of life.

Satan seems paralyzed. He had once been a covering cherub, and he remembers how much he has lost. He is forever excluded from the council where he once was honored. He sees another now standing near to the Father, an angel of majestic presence. He knows that the exalted position of this angel might have been his.

Memory recalls what heaven was like to him in his innocence, the peace and contentment that were his until his rebellion. He reviews his work among humanity and its results—the hostility of one person or group toward another, the terrible destruction of life, the overturning of thrones, the riots, conflicts, and revolutions. He recalls his constant efforts to oppose the work of Christ. As he looks at the fruit of his work, he sees only failure. Again and again in the progress of the great controversy he has been defeated and forced to yield.

The aim of the great rebel has always been to prove that God's government was responsible for the rebellion. He has led vast multitudes to accept his version of the great controversy. For thousands of years this chief of conspiracy has sold falsehood for truth. But the time has now come when everyone will see the history and character of Satan. In his last effort to dethrone Christ, destroy His people, and take possession of the City of God, the archdeceiver has been fully unmasked. Those who united with him see the total failure of his cause.

Satan sees that his voluntary rebellion has made him unfit for heaven. He has trained his powers to war against God. The purity and harmony of heaven would be supreme torture to him. He bows down and admits the justice of his sentence.

Every question of truth and error in the long-standing controversy has now been fully answered. The whole universe has seen the results of setting aside God's law. For all eternity the history of sin will stand as a witness that the happiness of all the beings God has created depends on the existence of His law. The whole universe, loyal and rebellious, with one voice declares, "Just and true are Your ways, O King of the saints!"

The hour has come when Christ is glorified above every name that is named. For the joy set before Him—that He might bring many sons and daughters to glory—He endured the cross. He gazes on the redeemed, renewed in His own image. He sees in them the result of the labor of His soul, and He is satisfied (Isaiah 53:11). In a voice that reaches everyone, righteous and wicked, He declares: "See the purchase of My blood! For these I suffered, for these I died."

Violent End of the Wicked

Satan's character remains unchanged. Rebellion bursts out again like a raging flood. He determines not to give up the last desperate struggle against the King of heaven. But of all the countless millions whom he has drawn into rebellion, none now follow him as leader. The same hatred of God that inspires Satan fills the wicked, but they see that their case is hopeless.

Fire comes down from God out of heaven. The earth is broken up. Devouring flames burst from every yawning chasm. The very rocks are on fire. The elements melt with fervent heat, the earth also, and the works that are in it are burned up (2 Peter 3:10). The earth's surface seems one molten mass—a vast, boiling lake of fire. "It is the day of the Lord's vengeance, the year of recompense for the cause of Zion" (Isaiah 34:8).

The wicked are punished "according to their deeds." Satan is made to suffer not only for his own rebellion, but for all the sins that he has caused God's people to commit. In the flames the wicked are finally destroyed, root and branch—Satan the root, his followers the branches. Evildoers have received the full penalty of the law; the demands of justice have been met. Satan's work of ruin is ended forever. Now God's creatures are forever delivered from his temptations.

While the earth is wrapped in fire, the righteous are safe in the Holy City. To the wicked, God is a consuming fire, but to His people, He is a shield. (See Revelation 20:6; Psalm 84:11.)

Our Final Home

"I saw a new heaven and a new earth, for the first heaven and the first earth had passed away" (Revelation 21:1). The fire that consumes the wicked purifies the earth. Every trace of the curse is swept away. No eternally burning hell will keep the ransomed thinking about sin's fearful consequences.

Reminder of Sin's Results

One reminder alone remains: our Redeemer will always carry the marks of His crucifixion, the only traces of the cruel work that sin has done. Through eternal ages the wounds of Calvary will reveal His praise and declare His power.

Christ assured His disciples that He went to prepare homes for them in the Father's house. Human language cannot describe the reward of the righteous. Only those who see it will truly know it. No finite mind can comprehend the glory of the Paradise of God!

The Bible calls the inheritance of the saved a "country" (Hebrews 11:14-16). There the heavenly Shepherd leads His flock to fountains of living waters. There are ever-flowing streams, clear as crystal, and beside them waving trees cast their shadows on the paths God has prepared for the ransomed of the Lord. Wide-spreading plains rise into beautiful hills, and the mountains of God lift their high summits. On those peaceful plains, beside those living streams, God's people, who have been pilgrims and wanderers for so long, will find a home.

"They shall build houses and inhabit them; they shall plant vineyards and eat their fruit. They shall not build and another inhabit; they shall not plant and another eat; . . . My elect shall long enjoy the work of their hands" (Isaiah 65:21, 22). "The wilderness and the wasteland shall be glad for them, and the desert shall rejoice and blossom as the rose" (Isaiah 35:1). "The wolf also shall dwell with the lamb, the leopard shall lie down with the young goat, . . . and a little child shall lead them. . . . They shall not hurt nor destroy in all My holy mountain" (Isaiah 11:6-9).

Pain cannot exist in heaven. There will be no more tears, no funeral processions. "There shall be no more death, nor sorrow, nor crying. There shall be no more pain, for the former things have passed away" (Revelation 21:4). "The inhabitant will not say, 'I am sick'; the people who dwell in it will be forgiven their iniquity" (Isaiah 33:24).

There is the New Jerusalem, the capital city of the glorified new earth. "Her light was like a most precious stone, like a jasper stone, clear as crystal" (Revelation 21:11). "The nations of those who are saved shall walk in its light, and the kings of the earth bring their glory and honor into it" (verse 24). "The tabernacle of God is with men, and He will dwell with them, and they shall be His people. God Himself will be with them and be their God" (verse 3).

In the City of God "there shall be no night" (Revelation 22:5). There will be no tiredness. We will always feel the freshness of the morning and always be far from its close. The light of the sun will be surpassed by a radiance that is not painfully dazzling, yet immeasurably exceeds the brightness of our noonday. The redeemed walk in the glory of perpetual day.

"I saw no temple in it, for the Lord God Almighty and the Lamb are its temple" (Revelation 21:22). The people of God are privileged to interact freely with the Father and the Son. Now we see the image of God like something in a mirror, but then we will see Him face to face, without a dimming veil between.

The Triumph of God's Love

God Himself has planted the loves and sympathies in human hearts, and in heaven they will find their truest and sweetest expression. The pure fellowship with holy beings and the faithful of all the ages, the sacred ties that bind together "the whole family in heaven and earth" (Ephesians 3:15)—these help to make up the happiness of the redeemed.

There, with delight that has no end, immortal minds will study the wonders of creative power, the mysteries of redeeming love. Every aspect of mind will be developed, every capacity increased. Learning will not exhaust the energies. The redeemed may carry on the grandest enterprises, reach their highest aims, fulfill their noblest ambitions. And still they will find new heights to conquer, new wonders to admire, new truths to comprehend, fresh objects to draw out the powers of mind and soul and body.

All the treasures of the universe will be open to God's redeemed. Not limited by mortality, they fly tirelessly to far-off worlds. The children of earth enter into the joy and wisdom of unfallen beings and share treasures of knowledge that these have gained through ages upon ages. With undimmed vision they gaze on the glory of creation—suns and stars and systems, all in their appointed order circling the throne of God.

And the years of eternity, as they roll, will bring still more glorious revelations of God and of Christ. The more we learn about God, the more we will admire His character. As Jesus opens before the redeemed the riches of redemption and the amazing achievements in the great controversy with Satan, their hearts thrill with devotion, and ten thousand times ten thousand voices unite to swell the mighty chorus of praise.

"And every creature which is in heaven and on the earth and under the earth and such as are in the sea, and all that are in them, I heard saying: 'Blessing and honor and glory and power be to Him who sits on the throne, and to the Lamb, forever and ever!'" (Revelation 5:13).

The great controversy is ended. Sin and sinners are no more. The entire universe is clean. One pulse of harmony and gladness beats through the vast creation. From Him who created all, life and light and gladness flow throughout the realms of limitless space. From the smallest atom to the greatest world, all things, animate and inanimate, in their unshadowed beauty and perfect joy, declare that God is love.

Sources

In the list below, under each chapter in the current work, are listed the source chapters in *The Great Controversy* that correspond to it:

Chapter 1, "Why Is There Suffering?"
   The Great Controversy, chapter 29

Chapter 2, "Hope for Triumph Over Evil"
   The Great Controversy, chapters 30, 31

Chapter 3, "Dangerous Seductions"
   The Great Controversy, chapter 32

Chapter 4, "Everlasting Life"
   The Great Controversy, chapter 33

Chapter 5, "False Hope"
   The Great Controversy, chapter 34

Chapter 6, "True Peace"
   The Great Controversy, chapters 7, 27

Chapter 7, "Our Only Safeguard"
   The Great Controversy, chapter 37

Chapter 8, "In Defense of the Truth"
   The Great Controversy, chapters 3, 25, 26

Chapter 9, "Real Hope"
   The Great Controversy, chapters 1, 17, 36, 38, 39

Chapter 10, "The Great Rescue"
   The Great Controversy, chapter 40

Chapter 11, "Victory of Love"
   The Great Controversy, chapter 42